LEADING FROM THE CENTER

LEADING FROM THE CENTER

Strengthening the Pillars
of the Church

WILLIAM J. WESTON

Geneva Press
Louisville, Kentucky

Book design by Sharon Adams
Cover design by Eric Walljasper, Minneapolis, MN

First edition
Published by Geneva Press
Louisville, Kentucky

This book is printed on acid-free paper that meets the American National Standards Institute Z39.48 standard. ∞

PRINTED IN THE UNITED STATES OF AMERICA

03 04 05 06 07 08 09 10 11 12 — 10 9 8 7 6 5 4 3 2 1

Library of Congress Cataloging-in-Publication Data

Weston, William J., 1960–

　　Leading from the center : strengthening the pillars of the church / William J. Weston.—1st ed.
　　　p. cm.
　　Includes bibliographical references.
　　ISBN 0-664-50251-2 (alk. paper)
　　　1. Presbyterian Church (U.S.A.)—Government. I. Title.

　BX8969.6.W47 2003
　262'.05137—dc21

2003040850

To

Margaret Blum Weston
Eleanor Hudson Weston
Samuel Josiah Weston

Contents

Figures

Foreword

*N*ot long after I was elected Stated Clerk of the General Assembly of the Presbyterian Church (U.S.A.) in 1996, a colleague shared with me a new book by William J. Weston titled *Presbyterian Pluralism: Competition in a Protestant House.*[1] He said that he thought I might find it helpful. If there was ever an understatement, his words that "I might find it helpful" would certainly qualify as such. I found Weston's analysis of the conflicts in the Presbyterian Church in the late nineteenth and early twentieth centuries and the rise of the "loyalist middle" to reclaim the church to be a most insightful framework for understanding American Presbyterianism. While the focus of that work by Weston was on the Presbyterian Church a century ago, I found his analysis to be a most helpful lens to understand church life as the Presbyterian Church makes its transition into the twenty-first century. The presenting issues of conflict were certainly different, but the human and organizational dynamics that he described from the early 1900s seemed to be very present in the Presbyterian Church at the end of the century.

I had the good fortune not only of reading *Presbyterian Pluralism* but also of coming to know William J. ("Beau") Weston and to benefit from his most helpful insights into the life of the church as it works through conflict. Weston is not only a distinguished professor of sociology but also a Presbyterian elder with a deep commitment to the life and ministry of this great church. I was one among many who strongly encouraged Weston to write a new book, taking this analysis and bringing it forward to our current situation in the Presbyterian Church (U.S.A.). He has done just that with *Leading from the Center*, and I believe this new book will prove to be a great blessing to Presbyterians who love their church as well as to scholars who seek to understand the dynamics of Protestant church life in America. While it is written with a specific focus on the Presbyterian Church, our situation is by no means unique as other mainline Protestant churches face similar challenges. I wholeheartedly recommend *Leading from the Center* not only to my fellow Presbyterians but also to all who seek the renewal of Christian denominations in twenty-first-century America.

Leading from the Center comes at a time when we really need it in the Presbyterian Church (U.S.A.). We have lived through well over a decade of intense conflicts between competing groups in the Presbyterian Church. There is a deep hunger for reclaiming the church's center and moving forward in faithfulness to the gospel among many Presbyterians. For others the deeper hunger is for an end to the conflicts that seem to be distracting our congregations from their more important work of proclaiming the gospel, celebrating the sacraments, and sharing the love of Christ with their members and communities. There are signs that the loyalist middle may well be reclaiming the church and seeking to chart its future. This book will be a source of inspiration and encouragement to that great body of Presbyterians.

In *Leading from the Center* Weston addresses today's constitutional conflict in the Presbyterian Church (U.S.A.) in the context of our history. He reminds us that we have never been a two-party church but rather one in which the competing sides seek to appeal to the loyalist middle—who, when the conflict is serious enough, rise up and set the course for the church. He cites the Adopting Act of 1729, which set the standard that church officers are to uphold the "essential and necessary articles" of our Confession of Faith, as a loyalist middle compromise between the strict constructionists and the loose constructionists who threatened division early in our church's history.

He again lays out in compelling terms the constitutional conflict of the late nineteenth and early twentieth centuries in the fundamentalist-modernist controversy. Again both sides were competing for the allegiance of the loyalist middle of the church, which emerged through the General Assembly Special Commission of 1925 and proposed a new consensus that was unanimously adopted by the General Assembly in 1927. That proposal, based on historic Presbyterian polity, both honored the evangelical faith of the church and the liberty of presbyteries to order the ministry without General Assembly–mandated "fundamentals."

Weston believes that the same dynamics are again playing themselves out in the Presbyterian Church in our time, and I think he is right. We are living in a time of intense conflict between competing sides over the presenting issue of ordination and human sexuality and, beyond that, over a range of theological and ethical issues. At the same time, there are growing signs that the loyalist middle is beginning to set the agenda for the church. As I write, we have recently completed the 214th General Assembly (2002) of the Presbyterian Church (U.S.A.), which by any measure would be deemed a loyalist assembly. The Assembly's major actions (which were all approved by large majorities) were to adopt a major theological statement on "Hope in the Lord Jesus Christ" to end a controversy on Christology among the competing parties; to launch a major Mission Initiative to support new church development and world mission; to trust presbyteries to enforce church discipline rather than intruding in judicial conflicts; and to refer a number of critical issues to the Theological Task Force on the Peace, Unity, and Purity of the Church (which is modeled after the Special Commission of 1925)—all strongly loyalist agendas! Given our history and our recent experience, based on Weston's analysis, we may well be seeing the emergence of the loyalist center's leadership in the life of the church. At least, that is what a Stated Clerk would hope for!

In addition to his very helpful sociological and historical insights, Weston's thesis also gives credence to a theological affirmation that has long been at the heart of Presbyterianism. Ours is a system based on the conviction that God indeed does work through the collective voice of the people and their spiritual leaders. A core Presbyterian principle is that the best way possible for human beings to discern the mind of Christ is not through popes, bishops, or potentates, but through the collective wisdom, drawn from prayer and the work of the Holy Spirit, of the elected spiritual leaders (the elders and ministers) of the people of God. It is a theological affirmation that God works through an empowered loyalist middle of the church, and it is encouraging to see that played out in the history of our church.

In short, I believe *Leading from the Center* is a seminal contribution to the future of the Presbyterian Church (U.S.A.), and I hope that it will be widely read and studied—and lived out in the collective experience of the church. While I do part company with Weston on some of his specific proposals for strengthening the loyalist middle (especially his assertion in Chapter 7 that "the Presbyterian Church does not have a confession" because it has moved away from a single confession to a *Book of Confessions*), I believe his basic thesis that constitutional competition can and usually does lead to a loyalist middle working out fresh compromises to empower the church's witness in a new generation is right on target and should be a source of real hope for a conflict-weary Presbyterian Church. I find this book to be stimulating and extremely helpful to my ministry, and I trust the same will be the case for you.

CLIFTON KIRKPATRICK

Acknowledgments

I first studied loyalist competition in the Presbyterian Church in *Presbyterian Pluralism: Competition in a Protestant House*, which was published by the University of Tennessee Press in 1997. I gratefully acknowledge the permission of the University of Tennessee Press to re-present some of the historical material that first appeared there.

This book brings together work presented over the past decade to a variety of helpful audiences, whose assistance I would like to acknowledge.

The International Society for the Study of Reformed Communities has heard preliminary versions of Chapters 5 and 6, which were published in volumes from those conferences: respectively, *Reformed Vitality: Continuity and Change in the Face of Modernity*, edited by Donald Luidens, Hijme Stoeffels, and Corwin Smidt (Lanham, Md.: University Press of America, 1998); and *Reformed Encounters with Modernity: Perspectives from Three Continents*, edited by H. Jurgens Hendricks, Donald Luidens, Roger Nemeth, Corwin Smidt, and Hijme Stoffels (Printed in South Africa, 2001). I thank the Society for their developed appearance here.

The book first took shape as a series of lectures to the Association of Stated Clerks in 2001. I am especially grateful for their hospitality and well-informed questioning.

Several friends performed the golden service of reading and commenting on the manuscript, by which it has been much improved. I thank Ron Afzal, of Sarah Lawrence College; Fred Beuttler, of the University of Illinois at Chicago; Robert Bullock, of *Presbyterian Outlook*; Joe Coalter, of Louisville Presbyterian Theological Seminary; Fred Heuser, of the Presbyterian Historical Society; Rodney Hunter, of the Candler School of Theology at Emory University; Jenny Stoner, co-moderator of the Theological Task Force on Peace, Unity, and Purity; and Mark Tammen, of the Office of Constitutional Services of the Presbyterian Church (U.S.A.).

Two of my main conversation partners, in print and in person, have been that excellent pair of jacks, Jack Rogers and Jack Haberer.

I owe a special debt of gratitude to Clifton Kirkpatrick, Stated Clerk of the Presbyterian Church (U.S.A.), for his continued conversation on strengthening the pillars of the church, for his helpful comments on the manuscript of this book, and for writing the Foreword.

Finally, I argued each point with my wife, Susan, the best interlocutor I could have, and I have inflicted the ideas of this book, as well as the time its production took, on my children, Molly, Nora, and Joe. To them this book is dedicated.

BEAU WESTON
Danville, Kentucky
August, 2002

Introduction

The Competitive Constitutional Church

Deep disagreements exist in the Presbyterian Church (U.S.A.) today. There have been deep disagreements for a long time. The issues change some, but the parties stay the same, and the fact of disagreement stays the same. Nothing short of the Second Coming is going to change that. We need to find a way to deal with the fact of disagreement that is in keeping with Presbyterian Church faith and practice.

Many people in the Presbyterian Church (U.S.A.) today fear that it is heading toward a split. Most church leaders think that a large schism is at least somewhat likely in the first half of the twenty-first century.[1] Several recent books by prominent church leaders, published by the Presbyterian Publishing Corporation, analyze the sources of division in the church in order to make a strong argument for unity. Jack Rogers, elected Moderator of the church in 2001, argues in *Claiming the Center* that competing worldviews are dividing the church, but can also be a source for reconciliation. Jack Haberer, former moderator of the conservative Presbyterian Coalition, argues that the church needs all of the five competing *GodViews* that he identifies. *What Unites Presbyterians: Common Ground for Troubled Times* is the unity-preserving case made by Stated Clerk Clifton Kirkpatrick and longtime missionary William Hopper Jr.[2] This book continues this line of argument.

The approach that I will argue for is that we should seek a "competitive constitutional church." I will explain what I mean at greater length below. The short version is that the best way to *contain* the deep disagreements that are endemic in the church is to let the opposing extreme parties compete for the central majority. The best way to *direct* that competition is if all parties adhere to the church's constitution, both the procedural parts and the substantive parts.

The Competitive Church

The thing we usually do in the church today is fight. These days this fight goes under the name of the culture war between the liberals and the conservatives, or progressives and orthodox, or whatever you call them. This is a strategy favored by conservatives, especially by the "angry young pastors" and by that unique polarizer, *The Presbyterian Layman*. People often say that, instead of this conflict, what we really should do is have a dialogue. Dialogue is a strategy favored by liberals, especially when they hold the institutional cards, as they have done for most of the past few generations.

Though conflict and dialogue are billed as opposite solutions to the problem of disagreement, in terms of social structure they are identical: two parties going head-to-head, polarizing the church. There are two problems with these two-party descriptions of what is going on in the church:

1. They aren't true.
2. They don't work.

When we actually look at the church we do not find it divided down the middle into two parties. Instead, we find a small left wing, a slightly larger right wing, and a large middle. The middle are not wishy-washy moderates, but a different party with a different agenda. The left tends to define the church by its ecumenical actions, while the right tends to define the church by its doctrinal purity. The center party are loyalists, loyal to the institutional church as it actually is. They are the people who say, "We've never done it that way before," and see that as an important argument. They are the defenders of constitutional practices, and mollifiers of all constituencies. Loyalists are maddening to prophets; they are the pillars of the church.

Loyalists have a historical and institutional conception of the church, and are loyal to their *particular* denomination, the Presbyterian Church (U.S.A.). Liberals may see the church as an institution, but their loyalty to the church in general does not keep them from exiting one denomination in favor of another. Conservatives may not even see the institutional church, but only its distinctive doctrines, and their loyalty to doctrine sometimes leads them to exit one denomination in favor of a new, pure sect.

Left and right elites like to talk about conflict and dialogue. They often really do see the church as divided into us and them, and tend to treat anyone who is not for them as against them. These elites also see a tactical advantage in getting people to talk about the church in *either/or* terms, in order to force those in the middle to choose one pole or the other. The extreme parties have permanent organizations and leaders and platforms and are in constant rivalry with one another. The loyalists, by contrast, do not have permanent organizations or articulated platforms. They desire the peace, unity, and purity of the church—*in that order*. Only in a crisis can they be mobilized, and only a crisis can call forth loyalist leaders.

For all their talk of conflict or dialogue, the extreme parties have almost no direct relations with one another. Instead, nearly all their effects on the church are mediated through their competition for the hearts and minds of the loyalist center. The loyalists hate to be forced to choose and thus divide the church. When they do choose, their choice is decisive for the church as a whole.

Loyalist competition is how the church works. Liberals, who enjoyed an almost unbroken dominance in the church for decades, have been faltering lately because they have not been getting this message. Though they keep winning battles, they are losing the war. In fact, one of the most intriguing findings of my survey of church leaders is that conservatives are much more optimistic about the future of the church than liberals are. Conservatives are pleased with the current conservative turn of church and society, are generally successful at keeping their own children in the denomination, and are hopeful about the future of the Presbyterian Church.

Liberals believe that they will eventually win on some of their favorite issues, such as homosexual ordination, but generally are less successful at keeping their children in the denomination, and are very pessimistic about its future. Liberals have become more extreme in their denunciations of the religious right, while conservatives have developed a whole panoply of organizations that eschew Presbyterian Lay Committee–style intransigence and seek to work within the system. The recent move of the denomination's top leadership away from the left and toward the center is a mark of this successful competition—meeting the loyalist majority where they are.

The church is better off because of competition for the center. The left and the right should be honored for keeping before the denomination some vision of the universal church.[3] However, if the left or the right ran the church, they would make drastic changes that would alienate many ordinary church people and destroy the denomination's actual structures. If the loyalist center ran the church alone, nothing would change because We've Never Done It That Way Before. Competition of the left and the right for the loyalist center assures gradual, organic, viable change in the church.

The Constitutional Church

A church is a large, diverse, complex institution. One of the main insights of the sociology of religion is that churches, as complex institutions, need rules and beliefs suited to a complex and diverse institution. In other words, a church needs a constitution.

The constitution of the Presbyterian Church has been one of its glories. The constitution today consists of the *Book of Confessions* and the *Book of Order*. To put it simply, the *Book of Confessions* contains the faith of the Presbyterian Church, and the *Book of Order* directs the practice of the Presbyterian Church. Both books are the result of centuries of wisdom and experience in running a national denomination.

The Presbyterian Church is more than a set of beliefs and rules; it is an institution. The church militant—the church in this world—must take some specific institutional form or other. Many have tried to create a "mere church" not tied to any specific denomination or polity. But real, concrete human beings cannot relate to one another in an abstract church in general. The church in this world will always have some kind of polity, some kind of constitution, be some specific kind of institution. This is not, in my opinion, a bad thing; it is not the result of the Fall. The institutional church is a necessary consequence of the fact that we are finite, concrete creatures who need finite, concrete institutions.

Sociology, more than other disciplines, is concerned with how institutions work, and the institutional form of a church—its polity—is vitally important to how it actually works. Institutions, in their real-life practices and effective beliefs, are what loyalists are loyal to. The Presbyterian Church takes its name from its polity, from its institutional form. The presbyterian form of polity is a middle position between congregationalism and episcopalianism. The Presbyterian institution was born of the ideological competition and literal bloodshed of the English Civil War. The Presbyterian Church as a functioning institution (that is, as a national denomination) is as much a product of centuries of wisdom and experience as its beliefs and rules are.

As an institution, the Presbyterian Church rests on the presbyter and the presbytery. The presbyter, or elder, comes in two varieties: (1) the teaching elder, or minister, and (2) the ruling elder, a layperson usually just called an elder. The local congregation is run by a session made of ruling elders, which is moderated by the pastor (a teaching elder). Above the congregation are the presbytery, the synod, and the General Assembly. At each of these higher governing bodies, a balance is maintained between the two kinds of presbyters.

The presbytery is the central institution of the Presbyterian Church. The presbytery is where the collective life of the denomination really lives. The clergy are not members of local congregations, as the laypeople are, but are all members of some particular presbytery. The presbytery is the equivalent of a diocese—a bishop's territory—in an episcopal (that is, bishop-led) church, with the presbytery as a whole acting as a collective bishop. The presbytery aids and oversees the individual congregations. The Presbyterian Church is not centrally run, nor is it decentralized down to each congregation. Instead, it has a connectional polity. The presbytery is where the organic connections of the denomination are largely forged and given life. The presbytery is where the Presbyterian Church's mission is determined.[4]

In England, after their Civil War, the episcopal party ultimately triumphed over the presbyterian and congregational polities. In the United States, by contrast, the decentralized, independent, congregational way has been very strong. The Presbyterian Church and our close cousins the Dutch Reformed (mainly the Reformed Church in America and the Christian Reformed Church) are in the minority among the heirs of Calvin in this country in retaining a presbyterian polity. Most denominations with Calvinist roots—the Congregationalists (United Church of Christ), the Disciples of Christ, the Church of Christ, the independent Christian Churches, and the many kinds of Baptists—all adopted a congregationalist polity. Indeed, in the southern United States, all churches seem to be drawn toward congregational independence, no matter what their official polity.

A magnetic pull toward congregationalism exists, even within the Presbyterian Church. Local freedom and local responsibility are very American. Since the cultural watershed of the 1960s there has also been more resistance to accepting any central authority in all kinds of institutions, including the Presbyterian Church. Perhaps most significantly, the vast majority of Christians live their church lives only in their local congregations. Only a minority of ministers will ever be commissioners to the General Assembly or serve on national church committees. The proportion of laypeople who are involved in the church even at the presbytery level is small, and the fraction active beyond that is miniscule. The General Assembly and the Presbyterian Center (church headquarters) in Louisville can seem very far away from the life of most Presbyterians.[5]

The Cooperative Consensual Congregation:
Why Can't We All Just Get Along?

Most members of the Presbyterian Church probably do not have much experience with the competing ideological parties in the church. They probably do not know much about the church's constitution, either. Most Presbyterians live their church life wholly in their congregations. They are often distressed by the perennial conflict in the church at the national level. More than that, they are mystified as to why there is such conflict when so little of that kind of conflict exists in their own congregation. They wonder why the Presbyterian Church as a whole cannot just get along, the way their local Presbyterian church does.

The answer is that any given congregation probably has less ideological disagreement in it than does the Presbyterian Church as a whole. Moreover, any given congregation is likely to suppress the ideological conflict that it does have, when dealing with matters in the congregation. These points are also findings of the sociology of religion. A diverse denomination is not equally diverse in each of its parts. Instead, a diverse denomination, like the Presbyterian Church (U.S.A.), is made of smaller units—presbyteries, congregations, and special interest organizations—that are themselves internally homogeneous. Furthermore, in a small, face-to-face group of people that lasts for years and years, people suppress their differences with one another in order to get along. It costs too much to have a feud with people you have to go on living with.

The ideal that many Presbyterians have is what we might call the cooperative consensual congregation. People cooperate because it is easier to get the work of the congregation done that way. The rules and beliefs that govern the life of the congregation have more to do with the consensus of the members than with the official rules and creeds of the denomination. It is often lamented that most Presbyterians do not have a deep knowledge of the Bible. This is doubly true about their knowledge of the church's confessions, order, and history. The average member of the church knows the working consensus of his or her congregation, and relies on the pastor and the elders to keep track of any parts of the higher governing bodies that might be relevant to the local church.

The Competitive Constitutional Church

The ideal for the congregation cannot be the ideal for the church as a whole. The church is larger and more complex than the congregation. The church has more ideological diversity, and less reason to suppress it. The church cannot simply rely on the consensus of the members, but must have a real constitution specifying the rules and beliefs—the order and confession—that actually constitute the church as an institution. The church as a whole cannot simply depend on cooperation to get things done. It needs institutional structures to let those with opposing views compete for the hearts and minds of the church's loyalist center. To be a competitive constitutional church is a good ideal for the Presbyterian Church (U.S.A.) as a whole to aim at.

PART I # How Did We Get Here?

Introduction

*T*he American Presbyterian denomination organized a Presbytery in Philadelphia in 1706 and a General Synod in 1717. The Confession, Catechisms, Directory for Worship, and Form of Government derived from the Westminster Assembly were, in practice, the guides for all American Presbyterians from the beginning. It was not until 1729, though, that they were officially included in the constitution of the church. The General Assembly for the new national church was created after the American Revolution in 1788.[1]

The constitution of this new national denomination, the Presbyterian Church in the U.S.A., consisted of the Westminster Confession of Faith, the Larger and Shorter Catechisms, the Directory for Worship, and the Plan of Government and Order, as amended by the church. The constitution established what had to be believed and done in the church, and the organization of the church as a system of courts meant that these constitutional standards of faith and practice would be enforced.

The Presbyterian Church in what is now the United States has always had a faction favoring strict construction of its constitution, another favoring a looser construction, and a large group in the middle loyal to church as it is. From colonial times, the strict constructionists tended to be Scottish and Ulster (Scotch-Irish) Presbyterians centered in Philadelphia and the regions to its west and south. The loose constructionists were more likely to be English Presbyterians and the small groups of Reformed Protestants from the continent of Europe. The Scotch-Irish tended to strictly insist on the creed of the church and the forms of Presbyterian religion, while the other group was less insistent on the Presbyterian distinctiveness and more concerned, in common with other churches, with the promotion of vital piety. While the ethnic character of these distinctions has diluted over the years, these different tendencies, in broad outline, remain. From the beginning, therefore, there was some diversity in the American Presbyterian Church.[2]

The competition between the liberals and the conservatives for the loyalist center of the Presbyterian Church is repeated in each generation. The meaning of "liberal" and "conservative" changes, but the basic parties are fairly constant. To better understand this competition in the church today, we can look back to a time with many parallels to our own—the fundamentalist-modernist competition of the 1920s. To lay the necessary groundwork for grasping that famous struggle, we will start with the heresy trials of the liberal Charles A. Briggs in the 1890s.[3]

Chapter 1

Too Big: The Inclusive Liberal Church of Charles A. Briggs

*C*harles Briggs was one of the leading liberal churchmen of the 1880s and 1890s. He was the Old Testament professor at Union Seminary in New York, then the leading liberal seminary of the Presbyterian Church. Briggs first provoked the ire of the conservative wing of the church in the 1880s by leading the charge to replace the Westminster Confession with a simpler creed. The confession was the core of the denomination's constitution and therefore dear to Presbyterian loyalists. Doctrinal conservatives opposed the new creed because they wanted to save distinctive Presbyterian doctrines, particularly predestination. Denominational loyalists opposed the creed because they thought it would be used as the "lowest common denominator" in a merger of many denominations, thus dissolving the Presbyterian Church altogether. Briggs maintained that his opponents were really motivated by the fear that creed revision would spell the end of the Presbyterian Church. He was probably right.[1]

The issue that got him suspended from the Presbyterian ministry, however, was not creed revision but his historical views of the Bible. When Briggs was himself a student at Union Theological Seminary, his professors urged him to go to Germany for further study, as several of them had done. Germany was then the center of the Higher Criticism of the Bible, which treated Scripture as the product of many literary traditions that had been combined during a long historical process. It was common for Protestant theological students to go to Germany from all over the world. Accordingly, in 1866 Briggs went to Germany. He did not take a degree, but spent several years attending lectures and study groups in several German universities. There he became convinced by the Higher Criticism, and made it his mission to bring it to the United States.[2]

After a brief pastorate, Charles Briggs began teaching at Union Theological Seminary in 1876, and from the beginning articulated Higher Critical views of the Bible. In the late 1880s he led the liberal group promoting a new creed. The two issues together led to Briggs's trials, which have been called the greatest heresy trials in American history.

Briggs's Liberal Vision of the Inclusive Church

Charles Briggs was an "inclusive" liberal in his conception of the church. He clearly articulates themes that we often see in liberal views of the church. He insisted on the orthodoxy of the Bible and the Westminster Confession, but also insisted that these historical standards allowed latitude for disagreement in interpretation. Briggs treated doctrine as the outcome of historical development, and his piety was of an evangelical type that emphasized Christian life over doctrine. Briggs took a Christian progressive view of history, arguing that Christianity and the church—of which the Presbyterian Church was only one passing form—would advance to ultimate triumph. Briggs's watchword for the church was "unity in diversity."

Charles Briggs thought that the church should be a "broad church," an institution in which a wide agreement on a small body of essential teachings would allow the acceptance of a great variety of views on other matters. He argued for this conception both as an ideal for the universal church and as a true description of the American Presbyterian Church, at least at certain points in its history. He described the original American presbytery as having a "broad, generous, and tolerant spirit," and he used this and other broad church phrases, such as "comprehensive," "catholic," and "progressive," to describe later developments in the Presbyterian Church.[3]

Briggs was willing to fight for toleration in the church, especially toleration for free inquiry. Free inquiry was an issue dear to his heart even before his suspension from the ministry, and he was willing to defend the rights of those whose views he disagreed with, such as the then-embattled scholars of Andover Seminary.[4] Though an ardent proponent of church reunion, he was even willing to delay the reunion of the northern and southern Presbyterian Churches if this would threaten the "tolerant and generous spirit" which the northern church had learned "in its treatment of error in useful evangelical ministers."[5] Note that Briggs is proposing not simply tolerance of *difference*, but tolerance of *error*.

Briggs thought that a modest view of what constituted the essential doctrines would restrain dogmatizing by allowing all manner of sinners to come into the church so that they might pursue sanctification, rather than requiring them to meet a high standard of perfection before they might be admitted. By treating most church practices as conventional rather than essential, Briggs's view allowed the church to more readily adapt to new circumstances. Briggs could sustain a modest view of the doctrines essential to the church because he believed that "Holy Scripture is for all alike . . . that all may maintain such sufficient understanding of it as is necessary unto salvation. Therefore a dogmatic faith is unnecessary unto salvation."[6]

Briggs took an activist view of Christianity, arguing that "[d]oing the teachings of Jesus is an ethical norm, corresponding with that of following him. This is not satisfied by merely recognizing him as sovereign Lord. Doing is the determinative factor and not merely professing."[7] This emphasis on work rather than doctrine is a characteristic feature of liberal thought in the church, often under the slogan, "Mission Unites, Theology Divides." The program of peace and work put forth by the liberals gave them common ground with the loyalists. Agreeing on work took the pressure off agreeing on doctrine, buttressing the argument that diversity of doctrine could be legitimate.

Briggs pioneered Presbyterian scholarship on the historical development of the church and its doctrine. This idea, so dominant today, was at the time a major departure from the prevailing view that the church could and did teach "the faith once delivered to the saints." In his *Biblical Study*, Briggs wrote:

> Experience shows us that no body of divinity can answer more than its generation. Every catechism and confession of faith will in time become obsolete and powerless, remaining as historical monuments and symbols. . . . Each age has its own peculiar work and needs, and . . . not even the Bible could devote itself to the entire satisfaction of the wants of any particular age, without thereby sacrificing its value as the book for all ages. It is sufficient that the Bible gives us the *material* for all ages, and leaves to man the noble task of shaping the material so as to suit the wants of his own time.[8]

This kind of thinking would later lead the church in the 1960s to drop the Westminster Confession and Catechisms as the one definite theological confession of the church, and instead adopt a whole *Book of Confessions.*

Briggs was committed to the church, but not necessarily to the Presbyterian Church. He contended that "Presbyterianism is not the last word of God to man. God has something vastly better for us than Calvinism."[9] Briggs favored the "comprehension" or inclusion of diversity in the church, a dynamic view that became the standard for the ecumenical program of the liberal party in the church. Briggs held that "[t]here can be no true unity that does not spring from . . . diversity. . . . If the visible Church is to be one, the pathway to unity is in the recognition of the necessity and the great advantage of comprehending the types in one broad, catholic Church of Christ."[10] Charles

Briggs's own inclusive vision went far beyond the Presbyterian Church, and beyond what moderate Presbyterians could accept for their church. "Denominationalism," he wrote, "is the great sin and curse of the modern Church."[11]

On January 1, 1891, a few weeks before he delivered the address at Union Seminary for which he was tried, Briggs published a clear statement of his vision of the church in "The Advance toward Church Unity":

> [I]t is only within recent years that liberty and variety have been won within denominational lines. This victory results in the decay of denominationalism; for in most, if not all, of the denominations there are those who break over the lines to the right and the left and clasp hands with kindred spirits in other denominations. The conservatives are, for the most part, denominationalists, but the progressives are indifferent to denominational difference, and are most interested in the progress of the Church of Christ as a whole. The progressives [in each denomination] . . . are now the most powerful parties. The only hope of conservatism is to unite the conservatives of all denominations against the progressives of all denominations. But so soon as this is accomplished the denominations will pass out of existence, and two great parties will divide Christianity between them. The old controversies are dead and buried; it is impossible to revive them. Those differences that gave the denominations their existence have lost their importance. . . . The signs of the times indicate that we are rapidly approaching . . . a crisis that will destroy denominationalism and make the Church of Christ one.[12]

These words of a century ago could have been written by liberals today. Liberals today are drawn to the view that there is a vast "restructuring of American religion" that will dissolve the old denominations.[13] If today they are not as likely to believe that "the progressives are now the most powerful parties" in each denomination, they often believe that history is on their side. Briggs makes the error here of treating conservatives and denominationalists as the same thing. Conservatives often agree with liberals that "the denominations will pass out of existence, and two great parties will divide Christianity between them." Loyalists, however, stubbornly preserve the denominations as the living form of the church. Activists, whether of the left or the right, who miss this point, often end up outside the church.

The Trials of Charles Briggs

The fight began in earnest in 1891 when Briggs was transferred to the newly created chair in Biblical Theology at Union, and in January of that year delivered his Inaugural Address, titled "The Authority of Holy Scripture." In this address he defended the authority and supernatural inspiration of the Bible, as well as the authority of the church and the "reason" (by which he meant experience and conscience, as well as reasoning). At the same time, he attacked bibliolatry and what he regarded as rigid and dogmatic versions of Calvinism. He used and defended the methods of Higher Criticism, and on this basis claimed that Moses did not write the Pentateuch and that Isaiah did not write most of the book that bears his name. Briggs emphasized God's immanence in the world, and proclaimed that there has been evolution in religious understanding.[14] Though this was not the first time Briggs had published his views, the Inaugural Address was widely publicized, especially by alarmed conservatives.

Conservatives considered these ideas, especially Higher Critical views of the Bible, to be heretical, and they demanded an investigation. In April 1891 they convinced the Presbytery of New York, of which Briggs was a member, to conduct a trial.[15] Following an investigation in October and November of that year, the presbytery voted that the charges were not sustained, and Briggs was acquitted.[16] The prosecuting committee, led by George Birch, however, took the matter to the denomination's General Assembly meeting in Portland, Oregon, in May 1892. Briggs claimed the prosecuting committee had no authority to continue after being dismissed by the presbytery, but the General Assembly allowed the committee to proceed. This Assembly, under conservative control, remanded the Briggs case to New York Presbytery for a new trial "on the merits." To make its own convictions clear, the Assembly also issued the "Portland Deliverance," which asserted against Higher Critical views the "inerrancy" of the original (and now unavailable) autograph manuscripts of the Bible, a theory propagated by Princeton Theological Seminary. Briggs and others questioned the constitutional authority of the General Assembly to make such a declaration on behalf of the church without seeking the concurrence of the presbyteries.[17]

In December 1892 Briggs was again tried in New York Presbytery and was again acquitted of all charges. The prosecuting committee then took its case back to the General Assembly, this time asking for an appellate trial by the entire Assembly. In so doing they bypassed the normal court of appeal, the Synod of New York. Briggs contested this, as well as again challenging the standing of the prosecuting committee after it had been dismissed by the presbytery. Nevertheless, the Assembly agreed to entertain the appeal, which it heard at the end of May 1893. Despite impassioned speeches on his behalf by other liberals, as well as Briggs's own erudite defense of his position, his victory in the lower court was overturned by a large margin. On June 1, 1893, Charles Briggs was suspended from the Presbyterian ministry.

At this same Assembly, the creed revision proposals that Briggs had championed went down to defeat. Briggs saw this as proof that his trial and the anti-revision effort were connected.[18]

The General Assembly of 1893 brought to a head a dispute between the denomination and Union Seminary. As part of the reunion of the New and Old Schools in 1870 the seminary had agreed to allow the General Assembly a veto power over the appointment of professors. The General Assembly of 1891 exercised this veto over Briggs's transfer to the new chair. Union Seminary contended that the right of veto applied only to new appointments, not to the transfer of existing faculty. The seminary denied the authority of the veto and abrogated the agreement of 1870. This issue was being discussed concurrently with the Briggs trials. After Briggs's suspension in 1893, however, the victorious conservatives demanded the capitulation of the seminary and the firing of Briggs. The seminary rejected this demand and returned to its original condition of independence from the General Assembly, retaining Briggs on the faculty.[19]

As the conservatives and the loyalists feared, Charles Briggs did indeed want to dissolve the Presbyterian Church into something broader. Briggs devoted the remainder of his life to promoting church union, a cause that had long engaged him, and became an acknowledged leader of the movement for organic union of all churches. He remained on the Union faculty until his death in 1913. In 1899 he was ordained in the Protestant Episcopal Church as a step on the path to a larger, united church, thereby becoming the first non-Presbyterian on the Union faculty. This brought some pressure on him to resign, but he was supported by liberals and ecumenists on the Union Board of Directors. Briggs remained a champion of the liberal Protestant church, and was one of the few Protestants with close ties to liberals in the Roman Catholic Church.[20]

The Consequences of the Briggs Case

The rules of the church require that ". . . when any matter is determined by a major[ity] vote, every member shall either actively concur with, or passively submit to such determination; or, if his conscience permit him to do neither, after sufficient liberty modestly to reason and remonstrate, peaceably withdraw from our communion, without attempting to make any schism."[21] When the majority decision went against him, even though he thought he had been railroaded and denied due process, Briggs did indeed withdraw quietly. Briggs himself remained in the Presbyterian Church for several more years before his ordination in the Episcopal Church. Somewhat less quiet were two other liberal scholars, Henry Preserved Smith and Arthur C. McGiffert, who were also forced out of the Presbyterian ministry in the aftermath of the Briggs trials, but they, likewise, did not attempt schism.

Henry Preserved Smith was a professor at the church's Lane Theological Seminary in Cincinnati. He was an ardent defender of Briggs within the church, and when Briggs went down, Smith went down with him. Smith was tried by the Presbytery of Cincinnati in 1892 for denying the inerrancy of the Bible and was suspended from the ministry. He appealed to the Synod of Ohio in 1893 and lost, so he then appealed to the General Assembly of 1894. Having suspended Briggs on largely the same charges the previous year, this Assembly had no difficulty deciding Smith's case. He lost by an even larger vote than Briggs had. Henry Preserved Smith joined the Congregational Church in 1899, and came to Union Seminary as librarian in 1913.[22]

Arthur Cushman McGiffert had been a supporter of Smith's on the Lane faculty. After Smith's suspension, McGiffert became the professor of church history at Union Seminary in 1893. In 1897 he published *A History of Christianity in the Apostolic Age*, which drew the charge from conservatives that he was irreverent and naturalistic in handling the Bible. When the matter came to the General Assembly in 1898 they attempted to avoid another heresy trial and encouraged McGiffert to withdraw quietly. McGiffert refused, denying that he had violated any essential Presbyterian doctrine. The Assembly of 1899 condemned views that McGiffert seemed to maintain, but the Assembly held back from naming him by name. In 1900, George Birch, Briggs's old prosecutor, brought charges in New York Presbytery against McGiffert. The presbytery condemned certain errors in McGiffert's teaching, but found him faithful to the church. Birch appealed to the General Assembly, where McGiffert was certain of condemnation and suspension. Before the trial, and on the advice of his colleague Briggs, McGiffert resigned from the Presbyterian ministry. He later joined the Congregational Church and, still later, became president of Union Seminary.[23]

The greatest long-term impact of the Briggs case on the development of the Presbyterian Church was that Union Seminary was freed from denominational control to become a leading center of liberal religious thought. This separation, brought about initially by the abrogation of the Assembly's veto power by the seminary, became part of the culture of the seminary with the addition of Henry P. Smith and Arthur C. McGiffert to the faculty, and through the movement, begun by Briggs, to make the faculty multidenominational. Though they were mutually independent, Union Seminary and the Presbyterian Church continued to have important effects on each other.

Briggs was removed from the ministry of the Presbyterian Church because his view of the church was so inclusive that it would have dissolved and destroyed the Presbyterian Church itself. Presbyterians loyal to the Presbyterian Church, understandably, did not accept this view. They were broad and tolerant within the traditions of the Presbyterian Church. They were not willing to use that same tradition of breadth to destroy the church. Briggs's completely inclusive view of the church was too big.

The removal of three liberal scholars—Briggs, Smith, and McGiffert—from the ministry and the defeat of the movement to revise the confession made the 1890s a very successful decade for the conservatives. They also counted the separation of Union Seminary from the denomination and the removal of the liberal voices at Lane Seminary as a gain. These latter events, however, would come back to haunt the conservatives, who thereafter had no direct leverage on the liberal intellectual centers. For their part, the liberal leadership was chastened by the disasters of the 1890s. They learned a greater respect for compromise and for the constitution of the church. For this reason, they had much greater success in broadening the institutional base of the church in the decade of the 1900s. Ultimately, the ability of liberals to compromise with the loyalists—and the rejection of accommodation by the conservatives—would mean the triumph of pluralism in the Presbyterian Church for a long time.

Chapter 2

Too Small: The Pure Conservative Church of J. Gresham Machen

*I*n the 1900s, the liberal leaders learned the lessons of Briggs's failures and grew more accommodating to the center of the church. As a result, they had a number of successes in that decade. In 1903 they led the drive to revise the Westminster Confession, softening the doctrine of predestination. This was much more successful than Briggs's attempt to completely replace the confession with a new creed. This revision led, as conservative opponents had feared, to a reunion with the less predestinarian Cumberland Presbyterians in 1906. The liberals also gave up on a denomination-dissolving merger of all the churches, and they instead led a successful movement to create the Federal Council of Churches in 1908.

In the 1910s the conservatives reacted to all this broadening of the church by narrowing church doctrine. The greatest achievement of this ideological retrenchment was the articulation of what were known as the five points or five fundamentals by the General Assembly in 1910, and their reaffirmation by the General Assembly in 1916. In these five points, the Assembly proclaimed that the inerrancy of Scripture, the virgin birth of Christ, his vicarious atonement, his bodily resurrection, and his miracles were all essential and necessary beliefs for Presbyterian ministers.

J. Gresham Machen emerged as a conservative leader in this period. Machen was a New Testament professor at Princeton Theological Seminary, then the leading conservative institution in the Presbyterian Church. He first became widely known in 1923 for *Christianity and Liberalism*, a strong argument that Christianity and an extreme form of naturalistic liberalism are really two different religions.[1]

John Gresham Machen was reared in Baltimore in the pious evangelical home of southern Presbyterians. Following a strong classical education in Baltimore, he entered Princeton Theological Seminary in 1902. He was a student and protégé of Benjamin Breckinridge Warfield, the conservative counterpart of Charles Briggs. Like Briggs, Machen was sent by his professors to study in Germany. He studied with the leading liberals in order to oppose their views and had a crisis of faith when he was unexpectedly impressed by their piety. Resolving this crisis, though, he came back to America convinced that liberalism of the kind he found in Germany was an alien religion threatening to take over the American churches.

In the fall of 1906 Machen returned to Princeton Seminary to teach New Testament. He remained in that position until he split the seminary in 1929, as will be described later. Though ordained, he never held a regular pastorate, and he was not involved in the regular institutional life of the Presbyterian Church outside of Princeton Seminary.

Machen became prominent as a conservative leader both inside the seminary and in the church at large with *Christianity and Liberalism* in 1923. In this and most of his subsequent work, Machen was at pains to show that liberalism was contrary to the historical understanding of Christianity and could in no way be considered orthodox. He was exasperated and offended that, as he saw it, such views were being propounded by ministers and officials of the Presbyterian Church. Two events in particular drew his ire: Baptist Harry Emerson Fosdick's preaching from a Presbyterian pulpit, and the Auburn Affirmation. The controversy surrounding these events served to form Machen and others of like mind into a self-consciously conservative party in the Presbyterian Church in the U.S.A. To religious conservatives of Machen's bent, the phrase "signer of the Auburn Affirmation" came to carry as much opprobrium as the phrase "card-carrying Communist" held for political conservatives of another generation.[2]

Machen's Conservative Vision of the Pure Church

The recurrent theme in all Machen's conflicts was that he saw the Presbyterian Church as a voluntary society teaching a pure doctrine, and he did not see how he could remain in the same body with people who did not agree with all of that doctrine.

Machen conceived of the church as an association for the teaching of Christian doctrine. This pure doctrine had its source in the Bible and its highest embodiment in the Westminster Confession, and it was not subject to change or development.[3] To maintain the purity of that doctrine, the church must be intolerant, exclusive, and free from the state. Therefore, when Machen spoke of the "church" he normally meant only the content of its teachings, rather than all the phenomena one might find in the empirical Presbyterian Church in the U.S.A. Machen considered his group to be the truly constitutional party in the church, but by "constitution" he meant only the sections dealing with doctrine, not the larger body of material on order, government, and discipline.

Machen clearly stated this doctrinal view of the church to the Thompson Committee when they investigated Princeton Seminary in the late 1920s (see the section on Machen's Schism in Chapter 3 for more background):

> The thing for which the Presbyterian Church exists, I hold, is the propagation of a certain doctrine that we call the gospel of the Lord Jesus Christ. . . . The Church might do many other things—it might tinker with social conditions, it might use all sorts of palliative measures with men who have not been born again—but only by persuading men to accept the blessed "doctrine" or gospel can it save human souls.[4]

The Presbyterian Church, in this view, is not defined by what it does in the world, by the religious experience of those within it, nor even by the form of government that gives the "presbyterian" church its name.

Machen explicitly rejected pluralism, both within the church and among religions. He claimed that:

> [a] true Christian Church is radically intolerant. . . . The Church must maintain the high exclusiveness and universality of its message. It presents the gospel of Jesus Christ not merely as one way of salvation, but as the only way. It cannot make common cause with other faiths. It cannot agree not to proselytize. Its appeal is universal, and admits of no exceptions. . . . Therein lies the offense of the Christian religion, but therein also lies its glory and its power. A Christianity tolerant of other religions is just no Christianity at all.[5]

Machen argued that a church, in contrast with the state, had a right to insist that those within it agree with all of its standards, and to remove any who did not. "Involuntary organizations," he wrote, "ought to be tolerant, but voluntary organizations, so far as the fundamental purpose of their existence is concerned, must be intolerant or else cease to exist."[6]

Machen had a conception of the church that was doctrinal, exclusive, intolerant, free, but not institutional. In his writings, doctrines were the actors, not institutions. Machen did not, of course, deny the existence or even the importance of the institutional aspects of the church; they simply did not figure importantly in his portrayal of Christian life. It was due, perhaps, to this view that Machen had relatively little experience with or responsibility for the institutional aspects of the Presbyterian Church. He had very limited pastoral

experience and gave little service to the committees and boards that constituted the nuts and bolts of denominational life. As a Christian, Machen's loyalty was to the gospel, rather than to the denomination, and therefore exit from
the denomination was relatively easy for him. When Machen began losing his
battles in the church, he began to speak openly of schism.

Machen's Critique of the Presbyterian Church

Machen criticized the Presbyterian Church on the grounds that it was liberal
and "nondoctrinal."[7] Liberals, in Machen's view, held that "creeds are merely
the changing expression of a unitary Christian experience, and provided only
they express that experience they are equally good." This made liberalism not
a variant or even a heresy of Christianity, but a non-Christian religion that was
attempting to take over the Christian churches.[8] In contrast with religious liberals, Machen opposed all attempts to reinterpret what he thought was orthodox Christian doctrine, or to unite denominations without full agreement on
that doctrine. Machen's battles in the church were as much over *whether* doctrine could legitimately be reinterpreted as over precisely *how* it should be
interpreted.

Having concluded that the Presbyterian Church contained two distinct religions, Machen naturally began to think about a division of the church. He
began publicly promoting schism in the church at least as early as 1923.[9] By
1936 he was ready to say that "[t]he Presbyterian Church in the U.S.A. is an
apostate Church at its very heart."[10] Toward the end of the 1920s Machen
began to think that it would be the conservatives who would pull out of the
church first,[11] and by 1933 he was avowing: "Certainly I do long for . . . a division in the present church. . . . The only question is whether that is to be done
by withdrawal of the Christian element . . . or elimination of the Modernist
element."[12]

Machen's conduct after that date seems designed to provoke his expulsion
from the church so that, as a "martyr," he might more effectively lead his party
out of the old church. He created an Independent Board of Presbyterian Foreign Missions specifically to provoke disciplining, because he thought that "if
we simply talk against the Modernizing agencies and do nothing about it, we
face no ecclesiastical penalties."[13] While publicly complaining about his trial,
privately Machen's only worry was that he would *not* be convicted: "Naturally," he wrote, "if anybody is to be a 'martyr' I should feel rather disgrun-
tled if I were not the one."[14] When Clarence Macartney offered to represent
Machen in his appeal before the Court of the General Assembly, "He

[Machen] replied with a kind letter, but declined my offer, saying that if I defended him, he might be acquitted, and that was not what he wanted." Machen said he feared that Macartney, a former Moderator and respected conservative, might get him off with a light sentence, and the issue would thereby be "evaded." Machen did not want that, because, he wrote, "I am longing for a division, and hoping and praying with all my soul that the division may come soon."[15]

Fundamentalists and Modernists Compete for the Presbyterian Church

In the 1920s the struggle between the liberals and the conservatives in the Presbyterian Church came to a head. On the whole, the liberals won. The conservatives had an early success in removing the liberal Baptist Harry Emerson Fosdick from a Presbyterian pulpit. However, when the liberals countered with a widely distributed plea for toleration and constitutional process in the church known as the Auburn Affirmation, the conservatives failed to press their advantage and try them in the church courts. The tide began to turn against the conservatives when the Special Commission of 1925 recommended toleration and unity in the face of disorder in the Presbyterian Church.

The first great struggle of the '20s was over the preaching of Harry Emerson Fosdick. Fosdick, a liberal northern Baptist, was one of the most eminent and successful preachers of his time. He was also a professor of preaching at Union Theological Seminary in New York when the First Presbyterian Church of New York City called him to be an associate pastor.[16] Since Fosdick was not a Presbyterian, this was highly irregular; by calling a non-Presbyterian, the liberals supporting Fosdick showed that they were not primarily denominational loyalists. New York Presbytery was generally tolerant of experiments, however, and the church was allowed to proceed. In 1922, though, Fosdick preached a sermon at the church titled "Shall the Fundamentalists Win?" Without Fosdick's consent, this was reprinted and circulated widely. It provoked the conservatives in the Presbyterian Church to action. Clarence Macartney, who published a reply sermon titled "Shall Unbelief Win?," led the opposition, with the assistance of Machen and others.[17]

Macartney and the conservative majority in Philadelphia Presbytery sent an overture to the General Assembly of 1923 to take action against Fosdick.[18] The anti-Fosdick forces lost the first committee vote on their overture, but impassioned speeches by Macartney and leadership by William Jennings

Bryan, the prominent Democratic Party leader and fundamentalist, won the vote on the floor. The Assembly ordered New York Presbytery to deal with Fosdick. To make their point clear, the conservatives succeeded in having the General Assembly adopt the five points—the inerrancy of Scripture, the virgin birth of Christ, his vicarious atonement, his bodily resurrection, and his miracles—for the third time.

Liberals and some moderates in the church had complained about the five points since their first proclamation in 1910. Some objected to the content, but more doubted that the General Assembly could, without the concurrence of the presbyteries, unilaterally enact what the critics called a new test of orthodoxy for the church. The reiteration of the five points by the Assembly of 1923 brought these questions to the fore again. When coupled with what was thought to be the prejudicial way in which Fosdick and the First Church pulpit had been treated by that same Assembly, these liberal and moderate elements were moved to produce a public plea for liberty in the church. The result was the Auburn Affirmation.

In early 1924 "[a]n Affirmation designed to safeguard the unity and liberty of the Presbyterian Church in the United States of America" was published from Auburn, New York. Part of the text was a protest against the treatment of Fosdick. The greater part, however, was about the five points. The affirmation protested against the constitutionality of the unilateral declaration of these points by the General Assembly. More important, it said that the points themselves were only one set of theories about the essential doctrines of Christianity. The document stated that while some of the signers did in fact agree with those theories, they all affirmed the liberty of interpretation that the Presbyterian Church had traditionally allowed on such matters. This appeal to Presbyterian tradition was designed to sway Presbyterian loyalists.

J. Gresham Machen was incensed by the affirmation. The affirmation, he argued, said that the five points asserted by the General Assembly were "only theories" and not a necessary belief for Presbyterian ministers. The virgin birth of Christ, Machen pronounced, is either a fact or not a fact; moreover, it is not possible to assert that one believes the gospel and yet treat its contents, such as the story of the virgin birth, as only a theory. Therefore, in his view, the Affirmationists were liberals of an extreme sort, blatantly professing their unbelief. Worse, by not disciplining them when it had the chance, the General Assembly acquiesced in this heresy.

In fact, however, the Auburn Affirmation did not simply draw a distinction between fact and theory; rather, it made distinctions among fact, *doctrine*, and theory. Speaking of the subjects addressed in the five points, the signers clearly stated: "We all hold most earnestly to these great facts and doctrines." They go on to say:

> Some of us regard the particular theories contained in the deliverance of the General Assembly of 1923 [that is, the five points] as satisfactory explanations of these facts and doctrines. But we are united in believing that these are not the only theories allowed by the Scriptures and our standards as explanations of these facts and doctrines of our religion, and that all who hold to these facts and doctrines, whatever theories they may employ to explain them, are worthy of all confidence and fellowship.[19]

It is not only the facts, therefore, that a Presbyterian must believe, but also the doctrines contained in the Scripture and the standards.

What is the relationship between a fact and a doctrine? This, it turns out, was a favorite topic of Machen himself. His usual illustration was this: "'Christ died'—that is history; 'Christ died for our sins'—that is doctrine."[20] A doctrine, in other words, explains the value of a fact. A Christian, Machen held, must believe both the fact and the doctrine. To this the Affirmationists agreed.

Accepting a fact and a particular interpretation of its value, though, still leaves a question of just how both fact and doctrine work, in other words, how they can be true. One needs a theory to explain the conditions of the world that make a particular fact and doctrine possible. To take Machen's example, the *fact* that Christ died and the *doctrine* that Christ died for our sins does not explain just how Christ's death can atone for our sins. One theory, the theory expressed in the five points, is that God accepted the crucifixion of Christ as a vicarious substitute for the sins of humanity. Some signers of the Auburn Affirmation also accepted this theory. This is not, however, the only theory, as the history of heated debates in the church over Christ's saving action testifies.[21]

The real argument of the affirmation, though, was not about facts or doctrines. The argument was not even about theories. Instead, it was about the constitution of the Presbyterian Church. Specifically, the affirmation contended that

> the constitution of our church provides that its doctrine shall be declared only by concurrent action of the General Assembly and the presbyteries. . . . From this provision of our constitution, it is evident that neither in one General Assembly nor in many, without concurrent action of the presbyteries, is there authority to declare what the Presbyterian Church in the United States of America believes and teaches.[22]

This concurrence of the presbyteries was never received, or even sought, by any of the General Assemblies that asserted the "certain theories" contained in the five points. Under the constitution, the Affirmationists argued, a Presbyterian had liberty to choose among several theories to explain the necessary facts and doctrines unless and until the Presbyterian Church judged among those theories in a constitutional manner.

The appeal to unity and constitutional liberty was a shrewd move on the part of the liberals: By convincing the loyalists that the conservatives posed a threat to the loyalist constitutional position, the liberals formed an alliance that also removed a threat to their own position. In saying that this appeal was "shrewd," I do not mean to suggest that the liberals were here disingenuous in their profession of loyalty to the constitution. Rather, I think that they were prudent in assessing the position of the Presbyterian Church at that moment. They stood a better chance of winning a case for liberalism under constitutional procedures than in a no-holds-barred fight. In other words, they stood to gain more by competition than by conflict. In the long run, they were right.

The affirmation appeared in early 1924 over the signatures of 150 Presbyterian ministers. By the time of the General Assembly of that year, nearly 1300 out of some 10,000 ministers of the church had signed it. Most of the liberals of the church signed, including its two principal authors, Robert Hastings Nichols of Auburn Seminary and Henry Sloane Coffin of Union Seminary. The signers represented almost every synod and the vast majority of presbyteries in the church, were less likely than the average minister to have come originally from other denominations, and were disproportionately pastors of congregations—the largest and wealthiest congregations at that. Moreover, while the liberal Auburn and Union seminaries provided the single largest group of signers, 14 percent of the total were graduates of moderate McCormick Seminary of Chicago, and a further 10 percent came from Princeton Seminary itself.[23]

The General Assembly of 1924

The appearance of the affirmation guaranteed that the General Assembly of 1924 would be a lively one. In retrospect, it appears to have been one of the pivotal meetings of the church in the past century. For the conservatives the Auburn Affirmation was a red flag of apostasy. Overtures were sent up from Cincinnati and Chester presbyteries demanding action against the Affirmationists. Another overture came from Philadelphia Presbytery raising the five points to be tests of orthodoxy for officers of the General Assembly. Finally, there was to be the further disposition of the Fosdick case, which the previous General Assembly had sent back to New York Presbytery for further treatment.[24]

The conservatives were organizing a campaign for Moderator of the Assembly, with Clarence Macartney as their candidate. The liberals did not run a candidate of their own, but quietly voted for the loyalists' standard-bearer, Charles Erdman.[25] Erdman was a professor at Princeton Seminary and a theological conservative. He was also, however, a man with wide experience in the Presbyterian Church, devoted to missions and church cooperation, and an ally of J. Ross Stevenson, the president of Princeton Seminary. In the seminary, Machen led the faculty "majority" in opposing the candidacy of his colleague Erdman for the moderatorship.

The election of the Moderator, the first important action of any Assembly, was a close one, but Macartney won. The principal committees chosen under his moderatorship had conservative majorities. Maitland Alexander, a strong Machen ally, was chairman of the important Bills and Overtures Committee, which decided where and how overtures should be treated. This committee had in its hands the Chester overture to take action against the Auburn Affirmationists.

The Assembly of 1923 had ordered New York Presbytery to treat with Fosdick. The presbytery had done so, but found him to be sufficiently orthodox and useful to the church to retain the First Presbyterian pulpit. Incensed, the conservatives returned to the General Assembly of 1924 demanding Fosdick's removal. The Assembly was stymied by the fact that Fosdick was not actually a member of New York Presbytery, and therefore not subject to Presbyterian disciplinary action. Before they could address the doctrinal question, therefore, the ecclesiastical issue had to be settled. To that end, the General Assembly sent down an order to ask Fosdick to either join the Presbyterian Church or resign his First Presbyterian pulpit.[26] When faced with this choice, the Baptist Fosdick said he could not affirm any man-made creed, including the Westminster Confession, and therefore First Presbyterian was obliged, reluctantly, to let him go.[27] The conservatives won the battle, but they were outmaneuvered in the Assembly on the organizational question and therefore failed to provoke a conclusive fight over doctrine.

The Philadelphia overture elevating the five points was sent to the Assembly's Permanent Judicial Commission. This body ruled that the overture was unconstitutional because it attempted to make a new test of ministerial subscription without the concurrence of the presbyteries. The conservatives lost again.[28]

The conservatives lost an important opportunity to press their doctrinal point in the Affirmationist case when they bypassed the central pillar of disciplinary order in the Presbyterian Church, the presbytery. Had the conservatives, instead of trying to act directly through the General Assembly, brought charges against individual Affirmationists within their presbyteries according to the usual order, they might well have won the substantive battle against liberal theology in the Presbyterian Church. The conservatives, attempting to go straight to the substantive point that they wished to establish, did not always attend to all the church's rules of proper procedure. They failed to see that for liberals, and especially for loyalists, the protection these rules gave to liberty in the church *was* the substantive issue.

In spite of these losses, it appeared to many that conservatives and their allies still held a dominant position in the denomination. Several observers, at both extremes in the church, thought the liberals, rather than the conservatives, would be forced to withdraw.[29] This estimate was especially popular before the Scopes trial of 1925, when fundamentalism was still a growing movement within the established churches, including the Presbyterian Church. To the surprise of many, though, it was the conservatives who eventually felt obliged to withdraw.

Chapter 3

Just Right: The Loyalist Constitutional Church of the Special Commission of 1925

*I*n retrospect, the General Assembly of 1924 seems to have been the high-water mark of conservative strength in the Presbyterian Church. The following year, 1925, was the year of the Scopes trial and a turning point for fundamentalism nationally. Within the Presbyterian Church it was also a year of arrested forward movement for the conservative program in the church. While the church was very far from becoming liberal, it did begin to move in the direction of toleration and breadth.

The first test of strength at the General Assembly of 1925 was the election of the Moderator. Charles Erdman of Princeton Seminary was once again the candidate of the loyalists and liberals, and this time he won a solid victory. The conservatives then won a point when the Judicial Commission ruled that New York Presbytery had acted improperly in licensing ministerial candidates who would not affirm the doctrine of the virgin birth of Christ. At this point, the liberals appeared ready to walk out.

To head off further acrimony, Erdman proposed from the floor that a special commission be set up to study the causes of the unrest in the church. They were to report to the next General Assembly "to the end that the purity, peace, unity and progress of the Church may be assured." This proposal was seconded by both Henry Sloane Coffin of Union Seminary, a leading liberal, and by William Jennings Bryan, the conservative standard-bearer who was soon to represent the fundamentalist side in the Scopes trial, and it was unanimously adopted by the Assembly. Erdman then appointed a Committee of Fifteen made up mostly of respected loyalists.[1]

The Special Commission of 1925, as this group is usually known, was faced with the daunting task of preserving the peace, unity, and purity of the Presbyterian Church in the U.S.A. in the midst of a competition so intense it threatened to tear the church apart. The loyalist center did not wholly agree with either the liberals or the conservatives, and were not ready to side with either. Moreover, they were sick to death of the constant quarrel. They wanted a solution to save the denomination.

The Special Commission's Loyalist Vision
of the Constitutional Church

In response to the continuing controversy in the church, the General Assembly appointed the Special Commission of 1925 to sort things out. It is fitting that, while the liberals and conservatives are represented in this story by two strong individuals, Briggs and Machen, the loyalists are represented by a committee. Briggs and Machen were each accomplished Bible scholars in a church that made scriptural study central, and they were effective polemical combatants who rose to leadership in their parties through personal initiative. The Special Commission of 1925, on the other hand, was composed of ministers and elders who had distinguished themselves by their devotion to the specific institutions of the Presbyterian Church in the United States of America. They did not put themselves forward for the role of judge in the conflicts of the church, but had the task thrust upon them.

The commission, appointed by 1925 Moderator Charles Erdman, consisted of eight ministers, seven ruling elders, and Stated Clerk Lewis Mudge, the denomination's highest administrator, who acted as secretary. Erdman also sat in on the discussions, although he did not vote.

The ministers were mostly long-term pastors of the denomination's leading "tall-steeple" churches:

- chairman Henry Swearingen (House of Hope Presbyterian Church, St. Paul)
- Mark Matthews (First Presbyterian, Seattle)
- Hugh T. Kerr (Shadyside Presbyterian, Pittsburgh)
- Lapsley McAfee (First Presbyterian, Berkeley)
- Harry Clayton Rogers (Linwood Boulevard Presbyterian, Kansas City)
- Alfred Barr (Chicago)
- Edgar Work (New York City)

The one exception was Rev. William Oxley Thompson, President of Ohio State University, who would go on to head the parallel commission sent to sort out the conflict at Princeton Seminary.

The elders were eminent professionals and committed laymen:

- vice-chairman Dr. John M. T. Finney (surgeon, Baltimore)
- Judge John DeWitt (Court of Appeals, Nashville)
- President Cheesman Herrick (Girard College, Philadelphia)
- Nelson Loomis, Esq. (Union Pacific Railroad, Omaha)
- President Edward Duffield (Prudential Insurance Company, New York)
- Nathan Moore, Esq. (Chicago)

The one exception was Robert Speer, Secretary of the Board of Foreign Missions and one of the most eminent bureaucrats in the church.

The placement of Speer and Matthews is most important. While there were no liberals on the commission, Speer was probably its broadest, most ecumenically-minded, and least denominational member.[2] As the undisputed leader of Presbyterian foreign missions, Speer would be the target of conservative attacks in the 1930s over modernism in the mission field. Matthews, on the other hand, was the commission's most conservative member, an avowed and militant fundamentalist who was sent by his presbytery to the General Assembly a record twenty times in thirty-eight years to "save the Church from the Modernists."[3] Whether he came down on the side of the ideologically-oriented conservatives or the institutionally-oriented loyalists would shape the conservative course in the church.[4]

At its second meeting, in December, the commission invited conservative leaders Clarence Macartney and J. Gresham Machen and liberal leaders Henry Sloane Coffin and William Adams Brown to address the group in individual sessions. The commission received several other testimonials and petitions, both written and oral, including a presentation by the Committee on Protestant Liberties in the Presbyterian Church. The latter was composed of the authors of the Auburn Affirmation and some of their supporters.

The conservatives maintained that the cause of unrest was that there was a naturalistic liberal party in the church that was not Christian, which was being tolerated by the sleeping majority of the church. The conservative solution was to make the Presbyterian Church take a stand on the essentials of Christian doctrine, thereby driving the liberals out. This was the strategy behind the five points.[5] The liberals, on the other hand, maintained that there had always been tolerance for diversity of opinion in the Presbyterian Church and that the problem came from dogmatic conservatives trying, unconstitutionally, to make everyone toe their line. This was the strategy of the "Auburn Affirmation."

The commission's Committee on Causes of Unrest and Possibilities of Relief partially agreed with each side. They agreed with the conservatives that the real issues in the conflict concerned different views on the Bible and the virgin birth of Christ. They agreed with the liberals that another real issue concerned the authority of the General Assembly to issue doctrinal deliverances, especially as they affected the ordination of ministers.[6] Against the conservative vision, though, the report states flatly that there is no naturalistic, Jesus-is-merely-a-good-man party in the Presbyterian Church.[7]

The causes committee took a distinctively centrist approach to what it viewed as the real issues. Whereas the liberals and conservatives thought the fight in the church was a substantive disagreement between two sides, the causes committee thought the problems arose because some were certain about the church's traditional doctrines while others were unsure. They urged that those ". . . whose minds are clear and definite may well exercise forbearance and charity toward those who are less able to affirm their faith in specific doctrines."[8] On the virgin birth issue, the committee claimed to speak for "a third party of large force in the church" that believed in the doctrine and would not debate it further, but thought that if ". . . there be reverent men among us, whose response is not clear on this point, let the church resolve that it will not harry them."[9] This is the kind of view that would lead Machen, whose particular specialty was the virgin birth, to tear his hair over loyalist "indifferentism."

Robert Speer summed up the loyalist view of the Presbyterian Church in the concluding section of the report. He wrote:

[T]he history of our church . . . has been a history of union, then division, then reunion. And unless we now face a new and different type of divergence we can only escape the principle of constitutional comprehension and of the union of hearts, in spite of divergence, by escaping from our whole history as a church.[10]

As the preceding section of the report had made clear, the committee did not think, as the conservatives did, that a "new and different type of divergence" existed in the church. The committee's position was that the church could solve its problems in the traditional way, by "constitutional comprehension" and the "union of hearts."

The Committee on Constitutional Procedure also took a loyalist, denominational view. Addressing the central issue in the five points–Auburn Affirmation dispute, they held that

it seems like trifling with sacred things to chance the fate of fundamental religious beliefs upon a mere vote of the General Assembly. An open and avowed change in the Constitution cannot be brought about without following a procedure which insures most careful consideration and action by the Presbyteries.[11]

The committee affirmed the authority of *presbyteries*, not the General Assembly, in deciding the qualifications of ministerial candidates. Most remarkably from a committee of which Mark Matthews was a member was the claim that "[i]n every presbytery there must be ministers who represent both schools of thought—the strict constructionist and the liberal construc- tionist," and the strong exhortation that modernists and fundamentalists try to agree on accepting ministerial candidates.[12]

The "Report of the Special Commission of 1925" to the General Assembly of 1926 perfectly articulates the loyalist position, the view that "constitutional comprehension" and "union of hearts" had always been and ought to be the Presbyterian way of settling disputes. The crucial section establishes tolera- tion on nonessentials as a fundamental constitutional principle of the Presby- terian Church:

> The principle of toleration when rightly conceived and frankly and fairly applied is as truly a part of our constitution as are any of the doctrines stated in that instrument. . . . Toleration as a principle applicable within the Pres- byterian Church refers to an attitude and a practice according to which the status of a minister or other ordained officer, is acknowledged and fellow- ship is extended to him, even though he may hold some views that are indi- vidual on points not regarded as essential to the system of faith which the Church professes.[13]

The commission proclaimed toleration in the church in a way that keeps the authority of the constitution foremost. More than defending toleration, though, the Special Commission report eloquently expressed the loyalist's devotion to the Presbyterian Church itself.

The Loyalist Majority Takes Command

The Special Commission of 1925 returned its report to the General Assem- bly of 1926. Taking a historical view of controversy in the church, it con- cluded that toleration would do more to settle the disputed issues than would schism. The limits of this toleration, however, would not simply be left up to individuals, but would be set by the church acting according to its constitu- tion. The General Assembly could not proclaim the essential and necessary doctrines of the church on its own, but could only do so with a concurrence of the presbyteries. The commission took a middle path between liberal claims for extreme toleration and the contention of conservatives, led by Machen, that there existed two distinct religions within the church, which should be separated from one another.[14]

The commission report was adopted by a sizable majority, and, according to one commentator, "satisfied all but the most extreme Fundamentalists."[15] The Special Commission asked for an extension to bring in their final report in 1927.

The General Assembly of 1927 began with an unusual event that signaled the revulsion of the center of the church at the prospect of division: the election of the Moderator by acclamation. Dr. Robert Speer was a highly respected loyalist who for years had run the foreign missions enterprises of the church. Under his moderatorship the Assembly of 1927 was one of the most united in many years.

When the Special Commission of 1925, of which Speer was a member, brought in their second and final report, the Assembly was ready for unity. The report stuck to the tolerant and mediating note sounded the previous year. It emphasized the necessity of strict constitutional order in the church and, for that reason, rejected the basis on which the five points had been declared. The commission's report was adopted unanimously and without debate.[16]

The tide had definitely turned against the conservatives. Thereafter the coalition of loyalists and conservatives that had, in the main, run the church since the Briggs trial came apart. This splintering was not over theological doctrine, but over church policy. The conservatives adopted a policy of doctrinal purity that did not fully reflect the actual historical diversity that had always existed within the Presbyterian Church. Perhaps more importantly the conservative position was out of accord with the constitutional safeguards protecting that diversity. The constitutional tradition, including the liberty that it allowed, was a defining part of the Presbyterian Church and, by the same token, part of the identity of those in the center of the church. The liberals had learned to respect the constitutional tradition, for if they did not, there would be no protection for the liberty that made their (minority) position in the church possible. When the conservatives took the extraordinary step of attacking and undermining that constitutional tradition—initially in the five points and Auburn Affirmation struggle, conclusively in the later Independent Board of Foreign Missions fight—they lost the competition for the hearts and minds of the center.

Thereafter the center of action in the Presbyterian struggle shifted from a fight between liberals and conservatives to a conflict between the center and the right. The most important battles of this struggle were fought in and about

Princeton Seminary. In these battles the loyalists would ultimately bring to bear the weight of the church, and the conservatives would withdraw from the seminary at the end of the 1920s. After a protracted struggle in the 1930s, this extreme movement would shatter, dividing and dividing again.

Machen's Schism: A Pure Seminary and a Pure Sect

In 1926, the year the Special Commission made its report, Machen was to be considered for promotion to the apologetics chair at Princeton Seminary. From a conservative perspective, Machen's uncompromising attitude toward liberal theology made him an excellent apologist for Christian doctrine. To the loyalists, however, Machen's threat to the peace and unity of the church made him the worst kind of apologist for the Christian church. The General Assembly, as had been demonstrated in the Briggs case, had a veto power over the appointment of professors in its seminaries, though it rarely exercised this power. The loyalist leaders at Princeton Seminary, President J. Ross Stevenson and Professor Charles Erdman, in a highly unusual move, urged the directors of the seminary not to promote Machen to the apologetics chair on the grounds that Machen was preset on a divisive policy, and Machen's "implacable hostility . . . would make brotherly cooperation . . . utterly impossible."[17]

When Machen's promotion came before the General Assembly, Stevenson urged that it and all other Princeton appointments be held up until a special committee could be sent by the Assembly to investigate conditions "subversive of Christian fellowship" at Princeton Seminary.[18] The Assembly, which had had enough of the festering divisions so publicly shown at the denomination's leading seminary, agreed to this proposal.

The Moderator of the 1926 Assembly, William O. Thompson, the president of Ohio State University and a member of the (ongoing) Special Commission of 1925, himself headed up the investigating committee. The Thompson Committee, which was made up of prominent loyalists, held interviews with all the groups at Princeton Seminary. They discovered that the faculty divisions were repeated among the Boards of Directors and Trustees, the director majority siding with the faculty majority, the trustee majority siding with Stevenson. The directors, who had charge of the running of the seminary, had been created by the General Assembly, while the trustees were a secular corporation that managed the seminary's property.[19] The two boards had clashed over the running of the school for several years.

The Thompson Committee found a wide divergence in the faculty over what the problem at the seminary was, as well as its solution. Machen and the faculty majority insisted that the root issue was doctrinal, but the minority insisted that there was no difference among them on doctrine. Machen said Stevenson was indifferent to doctrine, which Stevenson hotly denied.[20] The right wing of the church was splitting apart not directly over doctrine, on which they agreed, but on the importance of doctrinal agreement for the health of the church.

The issue on which the two sides were fundamentally at odds was whether the Theological Seminary of the Presbyterian Church in the U.S.A., as Princeton was officially known, should represent the whole church or only that part that had been in control at the time of the reunion of the Old and New Schools. Ultimately, the Thompson Committee, which itself represented the whole Presbyterian Church, concluded that "the drift of Seminary control seems to be away from the proper service of the Church and toward an aggressive defense of the policy of a group," and it came down on the side of Stevenson's representative vision of Princeton Seminary.[21] This position was in line with the policy of the Special Commission of 1925, just enacted by the church.

This still did not settle how the tension was to be reduced at Princeton. Even if the Committee had wanted to remove either faction (which it did not), such an effort itself would have defeated the attempt to make a representative seminary. Instead, the committee settled on the administrative (rather than doctrinal) solution of merging the two opposing boards of control and delaying the professors' promotions until that merger was accomplished. They reasoned that the division between the boards was what had made the seminary's other divisions interminable.[22] Merging the boards would force all sides to come to some sort of accommodation with one another. This solution would also allow everyone to save face by avoiding any question of the genuine orthodoxy of any party.

The administrative solution proposed by the Thompson Committee seemed to satisfy most of those concerned, but it deeply offended Machen and some of his group. They did not, it seems, want face-saving and accommodation; they wanted a showdown. Even when conservative leader Clarence Macartney tried to arrange a compromise whereby the promotions of Machen and another professor would go through in exchange for the conservative directors' acceptance of the seminary reorganization, it was Machen who opposed any compromise. The conservatives in the seminary vowed to fight.[23]

The Thompson Committee's report to the General Assembly of 1927 was well received. The committee then asked to be continued and expanded, so that it might settle the question of how, exactly, to accomplish the merger of the boards. In 1928 the expanded Thompson Committee brought in its report on how to merge the two boards. The new board, with a loyalist, pro-Stevenson majority, took control in the spring of 1929.

Machen thereupon withdrew from the seminary, taking with him four members of the faculty and some fifty students. He had already been raising money to start a new seminary, independent of denominational control. In the fall of 1929 Westminster Theological Seminary opened its doors in Philadelphia with a mission to continue the old Princeton Theology.[24]

Machen had wanted a showdown over doctrine, but what he got was a fight over order. Eventually, Machen made an all-out attack on the center in the church, leveling the most powerful charge that a doctrinal churchman could make against fellow clergy:

> The "heretics" . . . are, with their helpers, the indifferentists in control of the . . . Presbyterian Church in the United States of America, as they are in control of nearly all the larger Protestant Churches in the world.[25]

From this point on, Machen appears to have set on creating a schism in the church.

Machen chose his ground by attacking the church's Board of Foreign Missions headed by the guiding light of the Special Commission of 1925, Robert Speer. In 1933, Machen proposed an overture in New Brunswick Presbytery to make the foreign missions board reform itself and stop propagating error. No specifications of error were contained in the overture. The presbytery invited Machen and Robert Speer to discuss the soundness of the overture. After hearing both men make their cases, the presbytery declined to approve the overture, and instead sent one "affirming its confidence" in the Board of Foreign Missions.[26]

Machen's allies in Philadelphia Presbytery *did* pass the overture, however, and thus it was sent to the General Assembly.[27] At that Assembly Machen was invited to address the Foreign Missions Committee when it considered the Philadelphia overture. This was highly unusual because Machen was not a commissioner to the Assembly, no commissioner from Philadelphia would speak to the committee in favor of its own overture, and Machen's own presbytery of New Brunswick had specifically repudiated this same proposal. The *Minutes of the General Assembly* report that "[i]t was also known, as Dr. Machen himself later stated to the committee, that he would accept neither the judgment of the committee nor the decisions of the General Assembly if it did not conform to his view."[28] Machen was given an official hearing on his charges, while a representative of the Board of Foreign Missions "answered each point that he made one by one."[29]

Once again an official, and generally centrist, body of the church was not convinced by Machen's charges. In fact, the committee reported that both board and missionaries deserved the "whole-hearted, unequivocal, enthusiastic and affectionate commendation of the church at large."[30] The committee went on to say that, while everyone in the church had a right to criticize the church's representatives, it

> deplores the dissemination of propaganda calculated to break down faith in the sincerity of such representatives . . . [and reminds] every constituent of the Church that there are orderly methods of procedure whereby through the established courts all such representations ought to be made. The Assembly disapproves all methods of approach which would contravene such orderly methods, but would remind the Church that . . . a man must be held innocent until he is proven guilty of any charge; and that suspicion of motives is not adequate evidence against any man and certainly ought not to be used in the Christian Church.[31]

The full Assembly adopted this commendation, and the Philadelphia overture failed.

At the same General Assembly of 1933, Machen's allies on the Foreign Missions Committee had proposed an alternate slate of members for the Board of Foreign Missions. When their slate was rejected by the General Assembly, this group immediately declared themselves to be the Independent Board of Presbyterian Foreign Missions, with J. Gresham Machen as president.[32] The church's official account summed up this action this way: "In other words, the very persons who had asked the General Assembly to be given charge of the work of foreign missions and to whom the General Assembly had refused to entrust this work refused to accept the authority of the Assembly and proceeded to constitute themselves, in contempt of the Assembly's action, an Independent Board of Presbyterian Foreign Missions."[33] Denominational leaders were particularly irked that the new organization was created immediately, while the General Assembly was still meeting, evidently according to a premeditated plan.[34]

Since missions create new churches, the creation of a mission board independent of the denomination seemed to many to be schismatic and to require disciplinary action. While the church had come to accept independent seminaries, such as Westminster, it had specifically rejected working with independent mission agencies after long experience with them in the nineteenth century. The "Deliverance" of the General Assembly of 1934 on the Independent Board noted that the Presbyterian Church had tried outside missionary agencies for fifty years, but "experience had clearly demonstrated the inefficacy of such agencies under a Presbyterian form of government." An exception was made for "certain interdenominational work" that the church could not do alone and that the General Assembly had "approve[d] in specific deliverances." The Independent Board met neither criterion of this exception.[35]

In 1934 the Judicial Commission charged with interpreting the constitution took up the question; it ruled that the Independent Board undermined the good order of the Presbyterian Church. The General Assembly, in considering how to act on this ruling, was particularly provoked by the attempt of the Independent Board to get local congregations to divert their mission offerings from the official agencies of the church, already hard-pressed by the Depression, to this new board. Based on this judgment and evidence, the General Assembly of 1934 declared that officers of the Presbyterian Church in the U.S.A. must resign from the Independent Board or risk suspension.[36]

When the Independent Board members refused to comply with the directive of the General Assembly, proceedings were begun against them in their respective presbyteries. In 1934 and 1935, Machen was tried in New Brunswick Presbytery on several administrative charges, such as disobeying the orders of the General Assembly, advocating "rebellion" in the church, and refusing to abide by his ministerial vows in which he had promised "subjection to his brethren in the Lord." The members of the prosecution denied that there was any doctrinal issue in the case and affirmed their personal belief in the five points. Machen, on the other hand, charged that the real issues were not about administration, but doctrine, and he challenged every charge and every judge against him, losing almost every point.[37]

In March 1935, Machen had his day in court in the Presbytery of New Brunswick. Speaking through counsel, he refused to address the charges against him but instead tried to use his trial as a forum for attacking the doctrinal soundness of the signers of the Auburn Affirmation, the Board of Foreign Missions, and Princeton Seminary. He also denied the constitutionality of the General Assembly directive and the jurisdiction of New Brunswick Presbytery to try him. The court answered these attacks by ruling out of order any argument on the doctrine of the other groups (such as the Board of Foreign Missions) and by citing the Presbyterian rule that a lower governing body (a presbytery) cannot judge the actions of a higher (the General Assembly).[38]

The court heard the prosecution. The defense had planned to then make its case by showing Machen to be justified in his course due to the doctrinal unsoundness of other people in the church. When the court ruled that other people's doctrine was not relevant to the defense of Machen's own actions, Machen's counsel refused to offer any answer to the charges. The Presbytery of New Brunswick found Machen guilty and suspended him from the ministry, with the recommendation that the sentence not take effect until his expected appeals had been exhausted.[39]

Machen, along with the other Independent Board members, did appeal to the General Assembly in 1936, and they all lost.[40] In his appeal in 1936, Machen was given full opportunity to contest the constitutionality of the General Assembly's "Deliverance" of 1934 before the Permanent Judicial Commission. That body ruled against him and the other Independent Board defendants, and their judgment was ratified by the General Assembly by nearly a thousand votes.[41]

The conservatives had, of course, expected this. They were already organized for schism. In 1935, while the first trials were going on, a group of conservatives had formed the Presbyterian Constitutional Covenant Union in Philadelphia, to fight what they called Modernism, "Indifferentism," and majority tyranny in the Presbyterian Church.[42] In 1936, knowing that the General Assembly would rule against all the Independent Board defendants, the Covenant Union held its own meeting in Philadelphia. At this meeting they created the Presbyterian Church in America, today known as the Orthodox Presbyterian Church. J. Gresham Machen was the first Moderator. By the end of 1936 this new denomination had seventy-five ministers and about as many congregations in nine presbyteries across the country, almost all of which had come out of the Presbyterian Church in the U.S.A.[43]

It soon became clear, however, that Machen would not carry even the most conservative group with him into his new church. A number of the faculty and students of Westminster Seminary as well as several of his most prominent conservative allies within the Presbyterian Church in the U.S.A. declined to follow Machen into what they considered to be schism.[44]

Ironically, Machen was soon hoist by his own petard. Immediately after his separation from the Presbyterian Church in the U.S.A., Machen was challenged by an even more conservative group within the new Presbyterian Church in America. Rev. Carl McIntire led the premillennial dispensationalist fundamentalists against Machen. They believed that God had ordained a set number of ages, or dispensations, each with a different character, and by a careful correlation of biblical prophecy with contemporary events they judged that the last dispensation was near, when Jesus would usher in his thousand-year reign (the millennium). Machen did not agree with this view, but he was willing to tolerate it in the church.[45] He also disagreed with McIntire's claim that the Bible required the legal prohibition of all alcohol. The McIntire faction, which was strongly represented on the Independent Board, were not tolerant of disagreement, and they wrested control of the board from

Machen in 1936. Soon thereafter McIntire led a schism that split Westminster Seminary and Machen's church.[46]

On New Year's Day, 1937, J. Gresham Machen collapsed and died of pleurisy in North Dakota.

Consequences of the Special Commission's Compromise

By allowing competition within the constitution, the loyalist Special Commission of 1925 effectively ended the church's civil war and, despite Machen's best efforts, prevented a major schism. The center-right coalition that had run the church from the time of the Briggs case was displaced by a center-left coalition that has run the church up to the present crisis.

PART II   Where Are We Now?
                           _____

Introduction

*T*he Presbyterian Church (U.S.A.) today is in a season of intense competition between liberals and conservatives like the turbulence and tension of the 1920s and 1930s. In this part we will look at today's most intense and divisive conflict: the struggle over homosexual ordination. As in the earlier competition, the loyalist majority has been trying to steer a middle course between today's liberals and conservatives, a story that is only half finished.

One advantage that we have over earlier generations of Presbyterian leaders is that we can know much better, through survey research, what most Presbyterians believe and do. This statistical portrait will let us compare the middle of the church with the competing wings.

Much happened in the Presbyterian Church between the Machen schism and today. I will note only a few major structural developments that are crucial to understanding what follows. The northern church, the Presbyterian Church in the U.S.A., whose struggles from Briggs to Machen we have been following, merged with the smaller United Presbyterian Church of North America in 1958 to create the United Presbyterian Church in the U.S.A. (UPCUSA). In the southern church, the Presbyterian Church in the U.S., developments closely paralleled those in the northern church after the Second World War, though usually with a lag of a few years.

The '60s brought a cultural revolution in both churches, from genteel transformations in the 1950s, through the full boil of the late 1960s, to a simmer in the mid-1970s. As a result, women were ordained to all offices in the church, and racial ethnics, especially African Americans, were increasingly visible in the church and its concerns. Partly as a result of these cultural revolutions, the southern church suffered a major schism in the mid-1970s, which resulted in the creation of the conservative Presbyterian Church in America. Starting in the late 1960s, and also, I believe, partly as a result of these cultural revolutions, both churches began to lose members at a significant rate.

In 1967 the northern church wrote a new confession, the Confession of 1967. It also adopted a new theory of the place of confessions in the church's constitution. Up until then, the Westminster Standards had served as the church's theological constitution for over 250 years, with occasional amendment. With the Confession of '67, however, the church now adopted the theory that confessions were limited documents responding to their time. They were useful for general guidance but were not fully authoritative standards for interpreting Scripture or constituting the church. Therefore, the UPCUSA created a whole *Book of Confessions*, including the Westminster Standards, the Confession of 1967, and two Reformed confessions, another catechism, and a declaration. This downgrading of the constitutional authority of the confession meant, in practice, that thereafter most constitutional competition in the church would be over the *Book of Order*.

In 1983 the northern United Presbyterian Church in the U.S.A. and the southern Presbyterian Church in the U.S. reunited after a separation of nearly a century and a quarter. The new Presbyterian Church (U.S.A.) is in the process of creating new, united institutions. The church headquarters were moved from New York and Atlanta to combine in a gleaming new facility in Louisville, Kentucky. The church wrote a new Brief Statement of Faith, which is now included in the *Book of Confessions*. Two new catechisms have been created for use in the instruction of adults and children. The process of integration is well advanced. The church has continued to shrink. The number of affinity groups or special interest organizations devoted to various causes has grown. The leadership of the church, in my estimation, has made a noticeable move toward the center.

By 2001 the ideological competition in the Presbyterian Church had grown so intense that the General Assembly created the Theological Task Force on the Peace, Unity, and Purity of the Church. They face a task today similar to the one faced by the Special Commission of 1925. In this part we will look at the course of one conflict and at a picture of what is normal in the church as a way of understanding the challenges that the loyalist majority faces (and the materials it has at hand) in trying to rebuild the church's center.

Chapter 4

The Half-Finished Story of the Fidelity and Chastity Competition

The best way to see if loyalist competition is still driving the church would be to find an issue so divisive that the loyalist majority is forced to choose a direction for the church. No issue has been more divisive in the Presbyterian Church recently than homosexual ordination. This issue came to a head in the Presbyterian Church (U.S.A.) at the 1996 General Assembly and in the struggle over the fidelity and chastity amendment to the church's constitution. The story is not over, but the fidelity and chastity amendment—now section G-6.0106b of the *Book of Order*—is a milestone in the loyalist reassertion in the Presbyterian Church (U.S.A.) today.

The Presbyterian Church has maintained a consistent witness that homosexual behavior is a sin and that homophobia and civil discrimination against homosexuals are also wrong. In the past quarter century liberals have steadily increased their efforts to convince the church that homosexuality is not wrong, while conservatives, much less steadily, have been irritated by the church's support of homosexuals. Somewhat to the surprise of both sides, the church has not changed its position much on this issue despite increasing pressure from both wings and growing weariness in the center.

Definitive Guidance

Prior to their reunion in 1983, both the northern and southern branches of the church had a remarkably parallel pattern of pronouncements on homosexuality, and the currently united church draws from both positions. In 1970 the northern Presbyterian Church (UPCUSA) said that sex was good and from God, it should be kept in marriage, and the state should not interfere with private consensual adult sex, including homosexual sex. On homosexuality they said that " . . . [we] reaffirm our adherence to the moral law of God . . .

that . . . the practice of homosexuality is a sin. . . . Also we affirm that any self-righteous attitude of others who would condemn persons who have so sinned is also sin."[1] Here we see both sides of the church's position: rejection of homosexual behavior and rejection of the behavior of rejecting homosexuals. This is a classic loyalist position: loyal to the established ideas of the church, but also loyal to an already-existing group of people within the church. Above all, loyalists are devoted to the established procedures of the church, and if there are to be changes, they must be made "decently and in order."

In 1976 the UPCUSA reaffirmed that homosexual behavior is sin by turning down a homosexual candidate for ordination; at the same time, they appointed a two-year Special Committee to study homosexual ordination. This continued the church's pattern of balancing pronouncements and decisions about homosexuals: When one side has a victory, a conciliatory (or at least hopeful) gesture is usually made toward the other side. This reflects the loyalist concern with preserving the church as it is, including its competing wings.

The General Assembly of 1978 articulated the position that has been called the definitive guidance on homosexual ordination ever since. Accepting the human sexuality Special Committee's conclusions, the General Assembly declared: "[U]nrepentant homosexual practice does not accord with the requirements for ordination set forth in the Form of Government." The ordinations of previously ordained homosexual pastors, elders, and deacons were left standing.[2] Some conservatives wanted to send an amendment to the presbyteries to put this position in the *Book of Order*, but the loyalist majority were persuaded by Stated Clerk William P. Thompson that it would be better for the General Assembly to issue a definitive guidance in such a case than to single out a specific sin in the constitution itself. As usual, the conclusion that ". . . homosexuality is not God's wish for humanity"[3] was balanced by a reaffirmation that the church must welcome homosexuals and support their civil rights.[4] In 1982, the last year before the two branches reunited, the UPCUSA reaffirmed the definitive guidance of the 1978 General Assembly.[5]

At the same time, the southern Presbyterian Church (PCUS) also rejected homosexual ordination, yet it proclaimed in 1977 that the church should support homosexual civil rights.[6] This position was reaffirmed in 1978[7] and 1979.[8] The 1979 statement, while repeating that homosexual practice was a bar to ordination, was particularly open to the possibility of change on this point. This last point was made more forcefully and famously in 1980, when the General Assembly equivocally asserted that homosexuality "seems to be contrary to the teaching of scripture," but the church should be open to "more light" on what homosexuality is.[9] In the wake of that declaration, "More Light" has become a banner for congregations that accept homosexual practice.

The reunited Presbyterian Church (U.S.A.) quickly affirmed the positions of its two constituent branches. In 1985, the denomination's Permanent Judicial Commission affirmed that the definitive guidance against homosexual ordination was the law of the church and could not be ignored by congregations or presbyteries. The other shoe dropped in 1987, when the General Assembly asserted that the civil government should eliminate prohibitions on adult consensual sex and prohibit civil discrimination on the basis of sexual orientation.[10] At that same meeting an early attempt to add a fidelity and chastity amendment to the church's constitution was narrowly defeated, 286 to 265 (or 52 percent to 48 percent). Partly as a result of this vote, the Assembly passed (58 percent to 42 percent) a resolution that launched the Special Committee on Human Sexuality that made its fateful report to the 1991 Assembly.

The Special Committee on Human Sexuality was appointed by 1987 Moderator Isabel Wood Rogers, a generally liberal Christian Education professor. Early on, two prominent conservatives, Princeton Seminary professor Diogenes Allen and Eastern College president Roberta Hestenes, resigned, citing a liberal bias in its composition and mandate. Hestenes would later chair the 1996 Human Sexuality and Ordination Committee that produced the fidelity and chastity amendment. The 1988 Assembly asked its Moderator, generally conservative pastor C. Kenneth Hall, to appoint several replacements and additions to the Special Committee, to make it more balanced. When the majority of the Special Committee on Human Sexuality issued their controversial liberal report in 1991, these new appointees were the core of the dissenting minority of the committee.[11]

What did rank-and-file Presbyterians think, while all this high-level debate was going on? At the behest of the Special Committee, in June 1989 the Presbyterian Panel, the denomination's ongoing survey of the church, surveyed a representative sample of members, elders, pastors, and specialized clergy (i.e., ministers not serving congregations). The Panel revealed that a substantial majority of Presbyterians believed that sexual desire is good, yet three quarters of elders and members thought that homosexual, premarital, and extramarital sexual relations are wrong and that practicing homosexuals should not be ordained. Of the pastors, about half thought it possible to be a practicing homosexual and still be a good Christian, but two thirds still opposed homosexual ordination. Only among specialized clergy, generally the most liberal group in the church, did a majority accept homosexual practice.[12]

The Special Committee on Human Sexuality was sharply divided between a liberal majority and a conservative minority, each of which released a report in late February 1991. The majority report, *Keeping Body and Soul Together*, issued by eleven of the seventeen members, contended that patriarchal heterosexism is the basis of our society and that "justice-love," rather than purity, fidelity, or even biblical regulations, ought to be the Christian standard. Relying on scientific evidence as well as on theological and ideological analysis, the report addressed a variety of sexuality issues, including concerns with sexual abuse, marital violence, and the sex lives of older adults and the handicapped. The most controversial conclusions, though, were those in support of homosexual behavior and homosexual ordination. The majority report did not ask for immediate adoption of these conclusions, however, but only for more study of the issues.[13]

The minority on the Special Committee on Human Sexuality rejected these conclusions and issued its own report supporting biblical authority and the definitive guidance on homosexual ordination. Contesting the method of the majority, the minority report said that scientific findings about the natural basis of homosexual orientation do not determine the moral issue nor what the church ought to do about it.[14]

Keeping Body and Soul Together was generally greeted with consternation. It was the main topic of the 1991 General Assembly. The church's 171 presbyteries, including some liberal ones, sent a total of 85 overtures to the Assembly about the majority report, all of them critical.[15]

Moreover, the Ethiopian Evangelical Church Mekane Yesus, a Reformed and Lutheran church cooperating with the PC(USA), was "really shocked" by the majority report and sent a communication arguing that homosexual ordination was unbiblical. If the PC(USA) ordained homosexuals, it would "endanger the relationship between the two churches."[16] This communiqué introduced a theme that has since been important to the debate: that homosexual ordination would endanger the denomination's relations with its ecumenical partners, especially since the vast majority of third-world churches reject homosexual practice as unbiblical.

After an exhausting and much-extended debate, 95 percent of the Assembly voted to reject *Keeping Body and Soul Together*.[17] At the same time, the Assembly chose not to adopt the minority report. Instead, it asked the denomination's staff to prepare resources, including both reports, for a churchwide discussion. This material was to be sent with a pastoral letter, which affirmed that the Assembly had

reaffirmed in no uncertain terms the authority of the scriptures of the Old and New Testaments. We have strongly reaffirmed the sanctity of the mar-

riage covenant between one man and one woman to be a God-given relationship to be honored by marital fidelity. We continue to abide by the 1978
and 1979 positions of the Presbyterian Church on homosexuality.[18]

After the decision, Moderator Herb Valentine asked the commissioners to
reach out and pray for "those who continue to feel isolated after the action
of the Assembly." There was a silent demonstration by the proponents of
homosexual ordination, concluding with the demonstrators singing, "We Are
Gentle, Angry People."[19]

One of the most important incidents of the decade's homosexual controversy was the case of Jane Spahr, which came to a head in 1992. Spahr had
been ordained in 1974, when she was married and before the 1978 definitive
guidance decision. She subsequently divorced her husband, entered a committed relationship with another woman, and became a prominent avowed
lesbian. In November 1991, Downtown United Presbyterian Church in
Rochester, New York, called Spahr to their pulpit. Her call was protested by
ten churches and fifteen individuals in Genessee Valley Presbytery. The presbytery approved her appointment, but the complaint and appeal blocked her
from assuming her duties. On July 30, 1992, the Judicial Commission of the
Synod of the Northeast ruled 9 to 1 to uphold the call. This decision was then
appealed to the national level.

The Permanent Judicial Commission (the "supreme court") of the Presbyterian Church (U.S.A.) heard the appeal of the synod's decision in a marathon
five-day session, culminating on Halloween, 1992. They voted 12 to 1 to
reverse all the lower governing bodies and set aside Spahr's call, without
touching her ordination. The majority held that the synod had been too narrow, and the presbytery too permissive, in holding that the definitive guidance
did not apply since Spahr was not being ordained. The commission instead
said that since she was called to an office requiring ordination, the definitive
guidance did apply to the call.[20]

The Spahr case has become a much-discussed incident in the recent
struggle over homosexuality in the church because it bars an ordained minister from congregational ministry. At the same time, Spahr's ordination was
left standing due to a scrupulous reading of the definitive guidance and the
grandfather clause protecting those ordained before it. This kind of care for
due process is characteristic of loyalists devoted to the institution, even if it
produces ideological anomalies. The case has also been symbolically important because it meant that ministers were willing to break the unwritten rule
and sanction another minister.

The Spahr decision ensured that the 1993 General Assembly would be a
lively one. The liberal presbyteries sent twenty-three overtures, most asking

for local option on homosexual ordination, with a few calling for overturning the Spahr decision. Keeping pace, conservative presbyteries sent twenty-four overtures, mostly against local option and for definitive guidance on this issue.[21] The Assembly, by a 71 percent vote, declared the 1978 definitive guidance to be the "authoritative interpretation" of the church's standards. On local option, the Assembly affirmed that the presbytery's "inherent and unassailable powers of ordination" do not undermine the higher governing bodies' powers to "review and control" the decisions of the lower.[22] At the same time, the Assembly established a three-year, churchwide study of sexuality in general and homosexual ordination in particular. The Assembly voted not to let a group of homosexual dissenters speak, but conservative Moderator David Dobler took personal privilege to allow them twelve minutes. About one hundred people spoke or wished to, and many applauded them. After the final vote, about sixty people, carrying a pink triangle quilt and a cross, marched around the room for half an hour chanting and singing. Dobler asked everyone to stay seated and in prayer; only a few left.[23]

Although this Assembly strongly affirmed the ban on homosexual officers in the church, it also condemned Colorado Amendment Two, which proposed to drop "sexual orientation" from state antidiscrimination ordinances. The Assembly also directed the Stated Clerk to help end discrimination against homosexuals in the military.[24] Though the Orlando Assembly had a generally conservative tone, the loyalists in it drew the line at a very conservative overture from San Joaquin Presbytery to discipline the pro-homosexual More Light churches and encourage those who approve of homosexuality to leave the church. The Assembly said the overture "in tone and content, is not compatible with current church policy. . . . [and] stands in complete opposition to current church policy calling for hospitality toward homosexual persons."[25]

One unexpected event raised the stakes and activity before the 1996 General Assembly: the action of the General Assembly's Permanent Judicial Commission in the *Central Presbyterian Church of Huntington v. Presbytery of Long Island* case. In 1993, the pastor of one church said that her session had ordained a homosexual elder and a homosexual deacon. The session of another church (Central) asked the presbytery to review and correct the first church for violating church law. The Presbytery of Long Island first complied with this request, then retracted it, judging that such an investigation would hamper the ongoing churchwide dialogue on sexuality. Central appealed to the synod, which upheld the presbytery. The General Assembly's court upheld the synod, ruling that the presbytery acted within its discretion. The important part of this case, however, is not this decision, but the reasoning behind the concurrence offered by seven of the sixteen members of the Judicial Commission. They agreed with the decision, but said that both definitive guidance and authoritative interpretation were unconstitutional usurpations of authority by the General Assembly, since prohibiting homosexual ordination ". . . can in no way be considered to be an 'essential' of the Reformed faith and polity. . . ."[26]

This willingness of a large minority of the church's high court to overturn definitive guidance and authoritative interpretation led both sides to mobilize their presbyteries to overture the Assembly and formally amend the constitution.

The competition for the loyalist center headed toward a crisis.

General Assembly, 1996

Three candidates stood for Moderator, providing a textbook illustration of what "competition for the loyalist center" looks like. Rev. Norman Pott, pastor of First Presbyterian Church in San Rafael, California, announced that he was in favor of homosexual ordination. Rev. John C. Poling, pastor of First Presbyterian Church in Las Cruces, New Mexico, announced that he was opposed to homosexual ordination. Both were successful pastors, known in their presbyteries but not renowned in the church at large.

The third candidate was Rev. John Buchanan, pastor of Fourth Presbyterian Church in Chicago. Buchanan was already well known for his leadership in the partially successful reconciliation with the ultraconservative *Presbyterian Layman*, and even more so for leading the extraordinarily successful reconciliation after the controversial feminist Re-imagining Conference. Buchanan, basically a moderate liberal in most matters, had gone on record in favor of local option in homosexual ordination questions, leaving the matter to presbyteries and sessions to decide. In the moderatorial election, however, he declared that he would subordinate his own preferences in the matter, and he called on others to do the same in order to preserve the peace and order of the church. His slogan was "The Church Matters." A better statement of the loyalist position would be hard to find. Buchanan won on the second ballot, drawing 56 percent to conservative John Poling's 38 percent, with liberal Norm Pott far behind at 5 percent.[27] This result came even though, according to conservative estimates, liberal lobbying at the presbytery level had resulted in an unusually high proportion of commissioners—perhaps one fourth—being liberals.

About fifty overtures on human sexuality, equally divided between liberal and conservative positions, were referred to the Human Sexuality and

Ordination Committee of the Assembly. During three days of hearings and discussion, chairwoman Hestenes led the committee, by most estimates, with a fair hand but in a firm conservative direction. All parties in the committee agreed that, after twenty years of increasingly pitched debate, the church wanted decisive action on this issue. Before considering the overtures, the committee's daylong hearings had an overflow crowd of seven hundred and heard testimony from only half of the more than two hundred people who wanted to speak.

The committee passed the fidelity and chastity amendment, 26 to 17 (no abstentions). A second proposal to also send an amendment allowing local option on gay ordination failed, 18 to 31. The deciding argument was the Advisory Committee on the Constitution's contention that local option on ordination would be a far-reaching change that would undermine the connectional order of the church.[28]

The fidelity and chastity amendment passed by the 1996 Assembly reads:

> Those who are called to this office in the church are to lead a life in obedience to Scripture and in conformity to the historic confessional standards of the church. Among these standards is the requirement to live either in fidelity within the covenant of marriage of a man and a woman (W-4.9001), or chastity in singleness. Persons refusing to repent of any self-acknowledged practice which the Confessions call sin shall not be ordained and/or installed as deacons, elders, or ministers of the Word and Sacrament.

The amendment has several features worth noting. First, it says nothing about homosexual ordination—the very problem that brought it into being. Instead, the amendment tries to fairly regulate all ordinands' sexual behavior without singling out any sexual orientation. It would, of course, make homosexual behavior a bar to ordination, and for that reason it has been hailed as a conservative victory. The larger effect of the amendment, though, would be to raise the standard for the heterosexual behavior of the vast majority of church officers. Loyalists are uneasy about the absolute exclusion of any existing part of the church, even so tiny a minority (less than one percent[29]) as unrepentant, self-affirming, practicing homosexuals who aspire to Presbyterian leadership. Loyalists pushed conservatives to expand the fidelity and chastity rule to include all officers not only to be more fair, but also to prevent the divisive spectacle of prosecutors from one end of the church pursuing defendants from the other.

The second condition of the amendment—that "refusing to repent of *any* self-acknowledged practice which the Confessions call sin" (emphasis added) would be a bar to ordination—could require much more far-reaching changes in the life of the church than the fidelity and chastity condition. Though this clause is clearly secondary to the main point of the amendment, it became the primary point of discussion in the presbytery votes. The Presbyterian Church has many official confessions, most from the Reformation, full of little-studied sins that have long been dead letter. This amendment could create a multitude of new and difficult purity rules. Some of the newly important sins, such as the prohibition on usury, could be quite problematic for the church as it now is. For loyalists, some of these new or revived standards would be hard to accept. Even harder for them, though, would be to accept without specific discussion a general set of sins that might turn the church upside down.

The Human Sexuality Committee's report to the Assembly repeatedly emphasized their unity-preserving process. Roberta Hestenes opened, then called on Vice-Moderator (and liberal leader) David MacDonna, who stated that "the committee had a sense of integrity and honesty and had a clean feeling of unity even within their diversity." Moderator Buchanan asked all to pray silently for two minutes and to "ask oneself where might God be speaking to all of us on this matter."[30] Then they broke up into groups of four or five for twenty-five minutes to listen closely to one another, look for common ground, and write a brief group consensus, which was collected by the student assistants. Buchanan asked the commissioners to keep up the prayerful dialogue over lunch.

In the subsequent floor debate in the Assembly, only one change was made to the Human Sexuality Committee's statement: The phrase originally referring to marriage of "one man and one woman" was changed to "a man and a woman," in order to avoid any appearance of conflict with the church's policy accepting divorce and remarriage. The minority moved that its local option proposal be substituted for the main motion; this substitute motion was defeated. There was silence, prayer (led by Buchanan), and ten minutes of responses by those who felt injured by the pending decision. The amendment then passed by a vote of 313 to 236 (or 57 percent to 43 percent).[31]

The Human Sexuality Committee's report adopted the dual position that the loyalists had been struggling toward, trying to be true to the church's biblical foundation and its current institutional reality. It states clearly that

[h]omosexual orientation is not a sin; neither is it a barrier to ordination. However, the refusal to repent of any self-acknowledged practice that Scripture, interpreted through the confessions, calls sin, bars one from office. . . . Is homosexual practice sin? . . . Although it is not greater than any other, we believe that Scripture, as guided by the confessions, defines such practice as sin. . . . The foundational issue is biblical authority. . . .[32]

The committee argued that Presbyterians are always free to follow their consciences, but those who choose to be ordained church officers had thereby conscientiously chosen to exercise their freedom within the bounds set by the confessions' interpretation of Scripture. The committee rejected local option on the loyalist ground that it would be "a fundamental, far-reaching, and substantive change in the foundation principles of a connectional church . . . [because] [o]rdination is for the whole church."[33]

Following the familiar pattern of balance between rejecting homosexual practice ecclesiastically, while supporting it civilly, the Assembly approved a separate resolution "recognizing that committed same-sex partners seek equal civil liberties in a contractual relationship with all the civil rights of married couples," and it urged the Stated Clerk to explore supporting this stand. This resolution was approved 53 to 47 percent.[34]

Mobilizing in the Marketplace of Ideas

The action then shifted to the 172 presbyteries that had to vote on the fidelity and chastity amendment, quoted above, before the 1997 General Assembly. To become part of the church's constitution, the amendment would need a simple majority of 87 presbyteries. The competitors formed their mobilization strategies. In September the Renewal Coalition gathered publicly in Chicago. Coordinated through Presbyterians for Renewal, the meeting featured Roberta Hestenes, former Moderator David Dobler, and conservative pastor John Huffman, and it brought together some 450 people from various conservative groups to plan strategy.

Two months later a private gathering in Chicago, coordinated through McCormick Seminary, brought together about sixty opponents of the amendment, including several executive presbyters (that is, presbytery chief executives), to plan their strategy. In addition, Presbyterians for Lesbian and Gay Concerns (PLGC), the liberal Witherspoon Society, and a number of ad hoc groups joined this McCormick group in mapping an approach to the competition.

It soon became clear that the main fight over the fidelity and chastity amendment would not be over fidelity and chastity at all. Instead, the third sentence, barring ordination to "[p]ersons refusing to repent of any self-acknowledged practice which the Confessions call sin" became the center of the debate. The progressives took the offensive, charging that this sentence could lead to a legalistic inquisition into all sorts of obscure sins, which very few deacons, elders, or ministers could survive. The conservatives responded that this was a misreading of the amendment, which states that only the *unre-pentant* practice of *self-acknowledged* sins would prevent ordination. If the ordinand did not acknowledge a sinful practice, there could be no "inquisi-tion." More important to the conservative side, repentance is "the intent of the fidelity amendment," to take the title of a speech given in several places by Professor Fred Beuttler, the principal author of this sentence.[35] Both strategies play to the loyalist concern that this amendment, or any amendment, not require a great change in the church's practice.

The debate on the homosexuality issue was admirably civil. It was clear that many progressives did accept the premise underlying the 1991 document *Keeping Body and Soul Together* that homosexual practice could be just and loving. For this group the apparent biblical prohibitions were either misun-derstood or irrelevant, though they thought it tactically imprudent to say so. There was much less testimony by and about homosexual Presbyterians, which had been such a dramatic feature of previous General Assembly ses-sions on homosexuality. Instead, respectable liberal heterosexuals, usually married parents, led the opposition. They did not attempt to argue that homo-sexual practice showed justice-love, or even that it showed true fidelity and chastity. Instead, they attempted to neutralize the biblical condemnations of homosexual practice.

The biblical argument brought out an impressive array of theological tal-ent, on both sides. Prior to the General Assembly, "The Whole Bible for the Whole Human Family: Members of the Biblical Faculty of the Presbyterian Seminaries Speak to the Issue of Ordination" was issued over the signatures of thirty Bible professors at the denomination's seminaries; these signatories represented about half of the total number of Bible professors in the denom-ination's seminaries. They argued that the six passages in the Bible that appear to condemn homosexual acts are not really about sex but about other values such as hospitality, that the Bible writers may not have known about homo-sexual orientation, and that "the gospel of Jesus . . . invites gay and lesbian brothers and sisters to full communion in the church; it is the spirit of Jesus that calls and equips Christians for ministry; and it is the justice of Jesus that calls us to insure that those who are invited, called, and equipped are free to fulfill their ministries among us. . . ." They did not actually deny, however, that the Bible calls homosexual behavior a sin.[36]

The conservative reply was not long in coming. Conservatives pointed out that only five of the thirty signers were Presbyterian. Commissioners to the Assembly were given copies of "Responsible Love: A Response to 'The Whole Bible for the Whole Human Family.'" This document, also signed by thirty faculty members of Presbyterian seminaries, agrees that the Bible knows no homosexual orientation, but it also argues that the scriptural condemnation of homosexual practice, not any orientations of fallen human nature, determines how we should act. "It is not," they conclude, ". . . competent scholarship to assert that these texts are 'wrested out of context' when we understand them as a prohibition of all homosexual activity."[37]

Most of the debate turned on the third sentence of the amendment, concerning unrepentant and self-acknowledged practice of anything the confessions call sin. Probably the most widely read criticism of this part of the amendment was a "Letter to the Presbyterian Church (U.S.A.)" sent in a massive fall mailing to all ministers and sessions in the denomination. The letter was signed by fifty-seven prominent church leaders, including ten former Moderators, three seminary presidents, a former Stated Clerk, a number of tall-steeple pastors, and a leading pro-ordination evangelical (a coup for this group). The letter was careful not to be identified with any one person, organization, or location. It made the three points that would be featured in nearly all subsequent criticisms of the amendment: (1) that the confessions are full of unenforceable prohibitions, such as those on usury and "undue delay of marriage"; (2) that the amendment would lead to legalism and an inquisition of all potential church officers; and (3) that requiring compliance with the confessions, rather than merely seeking guidance from them, amounts to changing the officers' ordination vows. They concluded by saying that the signers do not all agree about homosexual ordination, but they do agree that this amendment is the wrong way to resolve the issue.

We can get a sample of the local debates by comparing two prominent presbyteries on opposite sides of this issue, Chicago and Greater Atlanta. On a snowy night in January 1997, with the national vote tied at thirty-seven presbyteries apiece, a crowd half again as large as normally attended presbytery meetings packed the church in suburban Oak Park, Illinois. This special meeting had been called for an evening so that "specialized" (nonpastoral) clergy, the most liberal voting group in the church, could attend. Speaking for the amendment were a conservative pastor, and Fred Beuttler, elder and Christian college professor who, as a commissioner to the General Assembly, had been the principal composer of the amendment. Speaking against it were Cynthia Campbell, president of McCormick Seminary, and William P. Thompson, former Stated Clerk of the northern Presbyterian Church and the original deviser of the definitive guidance formulation. The negative arguments followed the inquisition line of the "Letter to the Presbyterian Church (U.S.A.)," which they had both signed. The affirmative arguments emphasized that the intent of the amendment was to call all officers to repentance and not to single out any one sin.

In the responses from the floor it was clear that the two wings were talking past one another, and the loyalists in between were fearful that this change to the constitution would significantly raise the standards that church officers had to meet. The amendment was defeated by a two-to-one margin, one of the largest in any presbytery.

A month later the momentum had started to shift, and the national vote stood at fifty-two yea, forty-two nay. Greater Atlanta Presbytery, which was still recovering from an acrimonious decision to affirm the ordination of a minister who had changed sexes, packed a large church in suburban Dunwoody on a warm weekday. The presbytery committee had split four to four on the amendment, and the discussion, which had no designated leaders, went back and forth civilly. Frank Harrington, pastor of Peachtree Presbyterian Church, the largest congregation in the denomination, argued for the amendment on the grounds that it was time to end the acrimony, stand for morality, and uphold the standards of the church. He was followed immediately by Doug Oldenberg, the president of Columbia Seminary, who argued that the amendment should be defeated because ambiguity is better than bad law, and who stated that he himself was deeply ambivalent on the issue of gay ordination. After an hour the question was called, though many remained lined up to speak, because the familiar arguments had been run: Scripture, morality, and repentance on one side, freedom and witch-hunts on the other. The amendment passed, 55 percent to 45 percent.

The fidelity and chastity amendment passed on March 18, 1997, when it received the required 87th presbytery approval. The final vote was 97 presbyteries for, 75 not for. No longer Amendment B or the fidelity and chastity amendment, the text took its place in the *Book of Order* as section G (Form of Government)-6.0106b.

What Does This New Competition Tell Us about the Church?

On the issue of homosexuality, progressives and the conservatives have been operating from worldviews so different that each frequently does not understand what the other side is saying. To the conservatives, the Presbyterian Church is a fellowship of sinners who live within the Bible because it testifies to Christ, who alone can save them. To the progressives, the Presbyterian Church is a prophetic instrument for carrying Jesus' message of liberation that can save others. The progressives start from a belief that Jesus' message is equality, and they therefore see sexual practice equality as simply the next stage in the heroic march for justice that began with racial equality and gender equality. To conservatives, however, these three movements are not at all the same because the Bible says quite different things about each one, offering nothing against racial equality, a mixed message on gender equality, and everything against equality of all sexual practices.

The Presbyterian Church, however, has not been ruled by either of these visions. Instead, for a generation it has maintained a consistent loyalist witness on homosexuality. To loyalists, the boundary between the church and the world is crucial. Therefore, they see no inconsistency (and much practical merit) in following both a liberal policy of homosexual equality in civil society and a conservative policy of biblical authority in the church. As the dominant element in the church, the loyalist center has resisted quiet conservative attempts to exclude homosexuals from the church and to leave them unprotected in civil society. At the same time, though, the loyalist center has resisted increasingly vehement liberal attempts to normalize and validate the gay lifestyle in the church. Because both wings view the center as wishy-washy moderates, they have been continually surprised at how firmly the loyalists have maintained their position.

The Aftermath of G-6.0106b

Since the fidelity and chastity provision entered the church's constitution, there have been several efforts by liberals to dislodge it and by conservatives to strengthen it. In each case, the center held. The loyalists even managed to achieve a two-year "sabbatical" from any changes to the constitution about sex standards. As of this writing, there is a growing sense of hope in the center of the church that, perhaps, the great sex-and-Scripture struggle might get settled.

By the spring of 1997 it was clear that Amendment B, fidelity and chastity, would pass. Some liberal presbyteries quickly passed overtures to the 1997 General Assembly proposing a new amendment that would, in effect, gut the fidelity and chastity provision. The new fidelity and integrity amendment (Amendment A), passed the General Assembly by 60 percent to 40 percent. It was then sent to the presbyteries. It read:

> Those who are called to office in the church are to lead a life in obedience to Jesus Christ, under the authority of Scripture and instructed by the historic confessional standards of the church. Among these standards is the requirement to demonstrate fidelity and integrity in marriage or singleness, and in all the relationships of life. Candidates for ordained office shall

acknowledge their own sinfulness, their need for repentance, and their reliance on the grace and mercy of God to fulfill the duties of their office.[38]

Though promoted as a healing measure, this amendment infuriated conservatives by replacing the explicit language of "chastity" with the code word "integrity," a term sometimes used to name gay Christian groups. The presbyteries decisively reaffirmed the fidelity and chastity decision, defeating fidelity and integrity by a margin of 66 percent to 33 percent (114 presbyteries to 59). This was an even larger margin than Amendment B had had the previous year.

A few dozen congregations, and the Presbytery of Milwaukee, passed a "covenant of dissent" against the fidelity and chastity provision. Some vowed to defy the church and threatened to withhold funds from the denomination.[39] Similarly, though from the opposite end of the spectrum, the *Presbyterian Layman* urged withholding of funds if Amendment A passed. Stated Clerk Clifton Kirkpatrick described such tactics as "irresponsible" and urged the protesters to dissent using constitutional means.[40]

One longer term consequence of the Amendment A effort was the creation of a liberal umbrella organization, the Covenant Network of Presbyterians. About 8 percent of the church's ministers, and a bit under 2 percent of the church's congregations signed its "call to covenant community."[41] The co-conveners of the Covenant Network, John Buchanan and Bob Bohl, were former Moderators of the General Assembly and pastors of two of the largest liberal Presbyterian Churches in the country: Fourth Presbyterian in Chicago and Village Presbyterian in Prairie Village, Kansas, respectively. The Covenant Network and its conservative counterpart, the Presbyterian Coalition, have coordinated liberal and conservative strategy, respectively, in the subsequent competition over homosexual ordination and biblical authority. After the defeat of Amendment A, both John Buchanan (on behalf of the Covenant Network) and Jack Haberer (moderator of the Coalition) called for civility and opposed defiance and schism.[42]

In an extraordinary act of statesmanship, Stated Clerk Cliff Kirkpatrick convinced leaders of both the Covenant Network and the Coalition to join him in issuing a "call to a sabbatical" on divisive confrontations about sexuality. Issued just prior to the 1998 General Assembly, the "Call" sounded all the central loyalist themes. They appealed to all Presbyterians to

[h]onor and respect our Constitution (both the *Book of Order* and *The Book of Confessions*). Resist the inclination to develop further overtures to amend the constitution with regard to ordination and human sexuality. Resist the

inclination to provoke or initiate judicial confrontation. Make a fresh commitment to treat those with whom we disagree on these matters with respect, refraining from personal attacks, accusations, defamation of character or intrusive exposure of sexual orientation.[43]

Nonetheless, several overtures did come to the Assembly from the left and right, and some 90 congregations (out of approximately 11,200 in the denomination) had created a More Light Network that threatened to ordain practicing homosexuals in defiance of the constitution. The moderatorial election pitted Columbia Seminary president Doug Oldenberg, who had publicly opposed fidelity and chastity in 1996, against evangelical pastor Jim Mead, who supported it. Oldenberg won. Yet in one of his first acts, Oldenberg asked Mead to serve as Vice-Moderator. All through the Assembly, both men promoted healing and the "big tent" church. Even after the Assembly, Mead helped organize a conference on "Unity and Diversity" that featured a moving joint presentation by conservative Presbyterians for Renewal head Joe Rightmyer and liberal Presbyterians for Lesbian and Gay Concerns leader Scott Anderson. The sabbatical held.[44]

The General Assembly of 1999 was presented with a mess to sort out. Earlier in the year, the church's Women's Ministry Unit had provocatively announced that it was giving one of its "Women of Faith" awards to Jane Spahr, the lesbian evangelist whose judicial case had caused such a stir in 1992. Curtis Kearns, head of the National Ministries Division, which oversees the Women's Ministry Unit, rescinded the award, an action subsequently backed by the division's steering committee. The Executive Committee of the General Assembly Council, the church's elected governing body, then overturned Kearns's decision, on grounds that would appeal to loyalists: The award had been given following traditional procedures. When the full General Assembly Council took up the issue at the Assembly, it supported its Executive Committee in allowing the award—by one vote.[45]

The fragile peace of the sabbatical was threatened when a committee recommended to the Assembly that G-6.0106b be deleted from the *Book of Order*. However, the Assembly was swayed by the minority report of the committee to ask the church for two more years of study and discussion, instead. The minority report advocates offered arguments designed to appeal to loyalists. The Rev. Stephen Moss, primary advocate for the minority report, said in presenting it to the Assembly:

The minority report presents you with a simple and a clear alternative— have the quiet time that we need for civilized and thoughtful discussion, lis-

tening respectfully one to another, when we are not under the threat of having to vote on something, and maintaining our historic standard against
behavior that is contrary to Scripture, contrary to order, contrary to tradition, contrary to our constitution. Or, we can choose the way of the majority report. We can have ongoing, in your face dissention all across the
church for the next couple of years, and the "in your face" was what was
said in our committee. It's a clear choice. Don't lower the bar on behavior,
and don't lower the bar on civil discussion.[46]

The minority report was adopted, 61 percent to 38 percent. In response to
overtures condemning homosexual "reparative therapies," the Assembly took
the middle position, arguing that churches should neither require nor inhibit
them.[47]

In May 2000, the Permanent Judicial Commission (PJC) of the General
Assembly took up some long-simmering cases just before the General
Assembly and bent over backward to avoid a rupture in the church. In the
Hudson River Presbytery (or Dobbs Ferry) case, they allowed that churches
could perform same-sex holy union ceremonies, as long as they clearly stated
that these were not marriages, which have been consistently forbidden by the
church. In the West Jersey Presbytery case, the PJC ruled that the presbytery
could accept an unrepentant, practicing homosexual as an inquirer for ministerial ordination, as long as he was not allowed to go on to candidacy in
that state. In a pastoral letter to the church, Stated Clerk Cliff Kirkpatrick and
Moderator Freda Gardner emphasized that these rulings upheld existing
church policy.[48]

The 2000 General Assembly almost maintained the sabbatical, but at the
last minute, on a very close vote, sent another homosexual practice amendment to the presbyteries for a vote. The Assembly voted early on to continue
the sabbatical and defer all overtures about homosexual practice until the next
year.[49] An ecumenical pro-homosexual group called Soulforce staged a peace-
ful protest in front of the Assembly, inviting arrest of some eighty-one of their
number, including Jane Spahr and former Stated Clerk William P. Thompson,
author of the 1978 definitive guidance.[50] On the last night, the Assembly
passed an amendment, later known as O, that would flatly prohibit Presbyterian churches or clergy being involved in same-sex union ceremonies. The
proposal passed the committee by only three votes, and the entire Assembly
by seventeen (51 percent to 48 percent). A similar amendment had been
defeated in 1995.[51]

The Presbyterian Panel, the church's representative sample survey, gives
us a snapshot of church opinion on same-sex unions. When asked in August
2000, if "Presbyterian ministers should be prohibited from performing a

ceremony that blesses the union between two people of the same sex," 57 percent of members, 61 percent of elders, 50 percent of pastors, and 30 percent of specialized clergy agreed. Slightly higher percentages in each category agreed that same-sex union ceremonies should not take place in Presbyterian churches.[52]

Amendment O, though intended to prohibit same-sex union ceremonies in Presbyterian churches or by Presbyterian ministers, was much more broadly worded. This created problems for the amendment from the beginning. Predictably, the Renewal Coalition worked hard for the amendment and the Covenant Network worked hard against it. More unusual were open letters from the National Korean Presbyterian Council, representing 350 Korean American Presbyterian churches, supporting O, and another from nineteen liberal former moderators opposing it. Even the centrist *Presbyterian Outlook* issued an editorial against the amendment, arguing that it was too broadly written and could have consequences far beyond those intended.[53]

In the end, these unintended pastoral problems seem to have been decisive. Amendment O was defeated, 73 presbyteries for, 100 against.[54] This did not change the church's ban on same-sex marriages.[55]

The defeat of Amendment O, as well as some other challenges to traditional views in the church, led to the creation in several different places simultaneously of the Confessing Church Movement. One of the points confessed is that marriage between a man and a woman is the only appropriate context for sexual activity. This movement began in local churches, but it was spread nationally by the Presbyterian Lay Committee.[56]

With the two-year sabbatical over, the 2001 General Assembly was flooded with overtures, many seeking to overturn G-6.0106b. Jack Rogers, a well-known evangelical academic who had publicly endorsed homosexual ordination, was elected Moderator on a platform of "Confessions Matter." Early in the week, the Assembly voted to create a Theological Task Force on Peace, Unity, and Purity to try to address the several issues that threatened to divide the church. Some thought that the sexuality overtures would be referred to the Task Force. However, at the end of the week, the Assembly, by a vote of 60 percent to 40 percent, adopted a sweeping amendment that would strike G-6.0106b, invalidate the definite guidance and authoritative interpretation that had preceded it, and leave it up to local option to decide who could be ordained. The last point was embodied this way: "Their suitability to hold office is determined by the governing body where the examination for ordination or installation takes place, guided by scriptural and constitutional standards, under the authority and Lordship of Jesus Christ."[57] This proposed change in the constitution would go to the presbyteries, like fidelity and integrity in 1997, as Amendment A.

In December one of the most closely watched judicial cases petered out. First Presbyterian Church of Stamford, Connecticut, had called an ordained elder to a new term on the session. In the course of his examination, the elder, Wayne Osborne, admitted that he was homosexually oriented and was living with a man, but he declined to say whether the relationship was sexual. The session accepted this answer as within G-6.0106b's prohibition on "self-acknowledged practice" of what the confessions call sin. Osborne's installation was stayed, however, while a series of protests, judicial decisions, appeals, new hearings, and new appeals went up and down the church courts. By the time the General Assembly Permanent Judicial Commission ruled on the case, the session term to which Osborne had been elected was over. Therefore, the PJC ruled that the case was moot. It did not render a decision on how far a session must inquire about the practice of a church officer.[58]

At the end of 2001, at the beginning of the amendment voting season, the Presbyterian Panel revealed that nearly two-thirds of elders opposed Amendment A, while the ministers were evenly divided.[59]

Amendment A was defeated by mid-February 2002, about a month before the fate of the previous amendments had been decided. Some presbyteries, wearied of the endless voting on sex amendments, voted early and quickly on this one. The final tally was 46 for, 127 against (27 percent to 73 percent).[60] Moderator Jack Rogers and Stated Clerk Cliff Kirkpatrick sent a pastoral letter to the church in the aftermath calling for reconciliation.[61]

The General Assembly of 2002 was the most unified in years. In some ways it resembled the Assembly of 1927. To be sure, unlike the 1927 Assembly, there was a contested moderatorial election in 2002, but this ended in a loyalist way: The liberal and conservative standard-bearers were defeated by Fahed Abu-Akel, not associated with either party, who ran on a platform of hospitality. The Assembly called for a year of prayer for those who disagree on sexual practice issues. Called the Prozac Assembly by the *Presbyterian Layman*, the *Presbyterian Outlook* offered that it should be better understood as the "70–30" Assembly, referring to the lopsided votes by which it passed almost all of its business.[62]

The story of the competition over homosexual ordination and scriptural authority is not over. It is worth noting, however, that the pattern established by the center of the church in 1978, the year of definitive guidance, has held for a quarter of a century. Despite intense lobbying by both sides, the center has not budged—and the church has not divided. The official policy of the church remains faithful to traditional scriptural interpretation on homosexual practice but welcoming to members of all sexual orientations. The denominational loyalists have kept the line firm between the stricter policy that the church uses to regulate itself and the more liberal policy that it supports in civil society. The fidelity and chastity struggle may appear to be proof that the church is torn apart by conflict, but I see it as proof that the loyalist center is holding.

Chapter 5

What Is Normal in the Presbyterian Church Today?

*T*he loyalist majority is loyal to what is normal in the church, to the church as it is. People in democratic societies like ours often think that normal means "good"; strictly speaking, though, normal just means "what most people do." This is the sociologist's normal. The normal church, the loyalists' church, is the church of what-we-always-do. So, we must ask, what is the church really like now? Using survey data, we can get the big picture of what the church is like.

Let's start with a survey for you. How many of the following apply to you?

— College graduate or more in education
— Live in a medium-sized city or smaller
— Was not raised a Presbyterian
— Republican
— Attend church nearly every week or more
— Give 5 percent or more of your gross income to the church
— Pray to find God's will at least once a week
— Think your most important belief is knowing that God loves you
— Do not think the Bible is inerrant in every detail
— Think God's ultimate judgment will reward some and punish others
— Think nothing is more important in your life than faith
— Oppose the ordination of practicing homosexuals
— Do volunteer work in the community
— Have invited at least two people to come to church in the past year
— Think that being a Presbyterian is important to your Christian identity

According to the Presbyterian Panel, the denomination's excellent ongoing survey of church life, *all of the above are normal for most Presbyterians.*

The Panel consists of more than five thousand Presbyterian Church (U.S.A.) members, elders, pastors, and specialized clergy (that is, ordained clergy working somewhere other than in a congregation, such as teachers, chaplains, or denominational staff members). They were selected by the church's research service to give a representative view of the whole church, and the same group is surveyed repeatedly for three years, after which a new panel is made. We will be drawing our picture from the 1994–96 Panel, the most recent series that is readily available. One of the standard questions they ask is, "When you think of your theological position, which word or phrase best describes where you stand?" Figures 1–4 show the answers for each of these four groups from the 1994–96 Panel.

Figure 1: Members

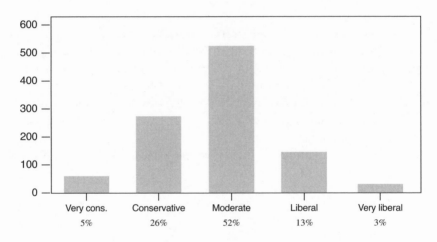

Figure 2: Elders

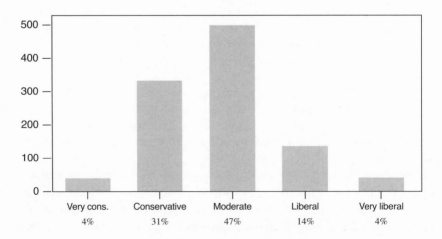

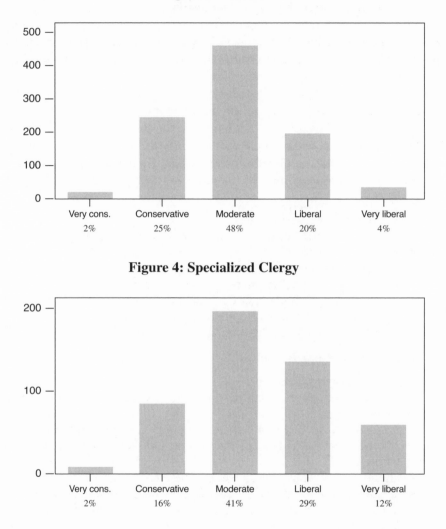

Figure 3: Pastors

	Very cons.	Conservative	Moderate	Liberal	Very liberal
	2%	25%	48%	20%	4%

Figure 4: Specialized Clergy

	Very cons.	Conservative	Moderate	Liberal	Very liberal
	2%	16%	41%	29%	12%

The elders, members, and pastors who make up more than 99 percent of the Presbyterian Church (U.S.A.) show the same pattern. About half are in the middle, tiny fractions are on each wing, and the remaining 40–45 percent includes somewhat more conservatives than liberals. Each of these groups is distributed across a conservative-leaning bell curve. The specialized clergy are somewhat different. They show a liberal-leaning curve, and their very liberal wing is not miniscule, as it is in the other groups. Though the specialized clergy make up about one-tenth of one percent of the church, they exercise an

influence all out of proportion to their size in their leadership of special interest organizations and in their votes in presbytery.

When we picture how the competition for the loyalist center of the church
works, it might be helpful to have these images in mind as a graphic reminder of
the two small wings competing to move the large, somewhat conservative center.

Members and Elders

Members and elders make up the vast majority of Presbyterians. Their char-
acteristics provide the baseline for what is normal in the church, against which
all other groups can be compared. Socially, most laypeople in the church

- are college graduates or better
- married to their first spouse
- have an executive or professional job, as does their spouse
- have two or three kids
- live in a medium-sized city or smaller
- know many or most of the people in their neighborhood
- do volunteer work for their community
- are twice as likely to be Republicans as Democrats
- are political moderates and reject the extremes

In their religious practice, most lay Presbyterians

- were not raised Presbyterian
- picked their church because it was Presbyterian or because a friend
  invited them
- joined because they found friendly members and meaningful sermons
- stay because it satisfies spiritual needs and they prefer a Presbyterian
  Church
- attend church nearly every week or better
- spend a fair amount of time at church besides worship services
- have invited two or more people to come to church with them in the
  last year
- give 5 percent or more of their gross income to the church
- attend Sunday school at least several times a month
- do volunteer work for their congregation
- pray to find God's will at least weekly
- are theological moderates and reject the extremes

In their religious beliefs, most lay Presbyterians

- say there is nothing more important in their life than their faith
- say the most important belief to them personally is knowing that God

loves them and the second most important belief is accepting Jesus Christ as their personal savior

- do not think the Bible is inerrant in every detail, but do think the Bible tells of God's involvement in creation
- do not think only church members can be saved, but do think God's ultimate judgment will reward some and punish others
- do not think all religions are equally good paths to truth, but do think the only absolute truth is Christ
- do not think evangelizing those who do not know Christ is "imposing" on them, but do think making a better society must start with converting people to Christ
- think Presbyterian Church (U.S.A.) affiliation is important to their Christian identity.

What most lay Presbyterians want the church to do is

- use churchwide offerings for disaster relief and meeting basic needs of the poor, not for "environmental justice" and the National/World Council of Churches
- call national staff to account when they publicly contradict official church positions
- oppose the ordination of practicing homosexuals
- give more attention to membership growth and decline, not to ecumenical issues
- give more attention to biblical faithfulness, not to social issues

In other words, most Presbyterians are solid upper-middle class family men and women, a little right of center in their politics, traditional in their piety, a little suspicious of change driven by the church elite, and loyal to their local church the way it is.

Presbyterian Clergy

Though the presbyterian polity gives elders an equal voice in church councils, the ministers—who make up less than one percent of the total membership of the church—have a predominant role in the denomination's day-to-day operations at every level and lead its factions at the national level. The clergy predominate because they have more training and knowledge about church affairs, have a high investment in their careers in the church, and have a permanent vote in the presbytery. The specialized (nonpastoral) clergy are particularly prominent in leading liberal movements in the church.

We will start our look at Presbyterian ministers with an examination of Presbyterian seminarians.[1] Presbyterian students at Presbyterian and non-Presbyterian seminaries are remarkably similar. The students at non-Presbyterian seminaries are more likely to call themselves evangelical than are students at Presbyterian seminaries, but they are just as likely to put themselves in the middle of the theological spectrum. The seminarians at non-Presbyterian schools were, not surprisingly, less committed to the denominational system; more surprising is the fact that they are also less committed to being pastors and more likely to plan to get a doctorate after seminary. In both kinds of schools, the conservative group is much more male than the liberals are. What is most surprising is that, aside from the theological differences themselves, there are no other significant differences, at either kind of seminary, among liberals, conservatives, and those in the theological middle.

The general effect of seminary education is usually to make graduates more liberal. The plurality who started seminary "middle of the road" theologically were twice as likely to become more liberal than to become more conservative. The seminaries differ significantly from one another in the theological distribution of their graduates who are Presbyterian ministers. The table below shows the Presbyterian seminaries, as well as the main non-Presbyterian seminaries that produce Presbyterian ministers.[2]

Figure 5: Theological Viewpoints of Presbyterian Ministers, by Seminary

Presbyterian	Very conservative	Conservative	Moderate	Liberal	Very liberal	Total
Austin	2% (1)	13% (6)	61% (28)	24% (11)	0	100% (46)
Columbia	1% (1)	23% (21)	51% (46)	20% (18)	6% (5)	100% (91)
Dubuque	4% (2)	33% (18)	46% (25)	15% (8)	2% (1)	100% (54)
Johnson C. Smith	0	25% (3)	50% (5)	25% (3)	0	100% (8)
Louisville	0	16% (14)	48% (43)	29% (26)	8% (7)	100% (90)
McCormick	2% (2)	7% (7)	51% (55)	30% (32)	10% (11)	100% (107)
Pittsburgh	2% (2)	25% (25)	51% (51)	19% (19)	3% (3)	100% (100)
Princeton	3% (6)	22% (49)	44% (97)	24% (53)	6% (14)	100% (219)
San Francisco	0	10% (7)	32% (23)	44% (32)	11% (8)	100% (72)
Union–Va.	2% (2)	6% (6)	65% (62)	20% (19)	7% (7)	100% (96)
Non-Presbyterian						
Union–N.Y.	0	4% (1)	35% (9)	50% (13)	12% (3)	100% (26)
Fuller	1% (1)	61% (42)	35% (24)	3% (2)	0	100% (69)
Gordon-Conwell	10% (4)	64% (27)	21% (9)	5% (2)	0	100% (42)
Total	2%	22%	46%	23%	6%	100%

After graduation from seminary, those who change their theological position are likely to become more conservative. I cannot tell from this survey why some ministers change their positions, but changes in marriage and family life clearly seem to be an important factor. One of the most striking differences among Presbyterian ministers that develop after seminary is the ratio of married to divorced people in different groups. Among theological conservatives, there are 89 married ministers for every divorced one; for those in the center the ratio is 16 to one; for liberals, there are 7.7 married people for each divorced person. An extraordinary extension of this pattern is that for ministers in church agencies or governing bodies (that is, presbyteries, synods, or General-Assembly-level bodies), the married-to-divorced ratio is 2.2 to one.[3]

Presbyterian ministers are mostly pastors of congregations under 300 members in medium-sized cities or smaller. Most are married baby boomer men with small families. They are in the middle of the theological spectrum, committed to the local ministry, and strongly committed to the denominational system. The conservatives are more likely to be small-town, small-church pastors, significantly more likely to be men and fathers, and much more likely to be in their first marriage. The conservatives are more committed to local ministry and less committed to the denominational system. As we saw in the opening bar graphs, most pastors are in the theological center of the church, with a lean to the conservative side.

Very Conservative and Very Liberal

Among members and elders, the Presbyterian Church's far right—the 3 or 4 percent who call themselves very conservative theologically—is surprisingly similar to the church's norm, with the exception of a few defining conservative beliefs.[4] They are much more likely to be Republicans and call themselves political conservatives than do most members, and they are a little less educated and less likely to have professional or executive jobs.

Otherwise, though, the very conservative are quite close to the social norms of the church. In their religious practices they are above the average on all counts, and they are notably more likely to give to their congregation. In their religious beliefs they only differ strikingly from the rest of the church in their acceptance of the idea that the Bible is inerrant and that no one outside the church can be saved. While strongly committed to the practices and most of the doctrines of the Presbyterian Church, they seem a little less attached to the actual denomination than some other groups. They have a relatively low commitment to the idea that their Presbyterian Church affiliation is important to their Christian identity; whereas most members and leaders rank their preference for the Presbyterian Church as one of the two main reasons they stay with their congregation, the far right ranked that reason eighth.

The far left of the Presbyterian Church—the 4 to 5 percent who call themselves very liberal theologically—is strikingly different from all the other groups considered thus far. Socially, they are more educated, more professional, better paid, more urban, more divorced, and much more Democratic than the Presbyterian norm. They are below average in attending worship, spending time at the church, volunteering for the congregation, inviting friends to worship, and giving to the church. Whereas most Presbyterians named knowing that Christ was their savior their second most important article of faith, the far left listed "helping others" second; Christ as savior was eighth.

Very liberal Presbyterians are quite different from other Presbyterians in some traditional Christian beliefs. They do not believe in divine judgment or that Christ is the only absolute truth; they do believe that evangelizing the unchurched is imposing on them. Given these deviations, it is not surprising that the far left does not seem as attached to the Presbyterian Church as others are. Whereas most members name their preference for the Presbyterian Church as one of the two main reasons they stay with their congregation, very liberal Presbyterians rank that reason fifth.

What is surprising is that the far left is the most likely of any group yet considered to say that their affiliation with the Presbyterian Church is an important part of their Christian identity. This last point raises a fundamental question for our consideration of loyalist competition in the church: If the people on the extremes are so different from the norm, why do they stay?

For the far right, this question is not so hard to answer because, as we have seen, they do not differ much from the norm of the church except on a few defining doctrinal points. Their experience in the Presbyterian Church is not very dissonant in either social or church practice. For the far left, on the other hand, their dissonance (and dissidence) from the norm is great.

One answer may be that those on the extremes stay because the Presbyterian Church is all they have ever known. Most Presbyterians, including most lay leaders and clergy leaders, were not born Presbyterians but instead chose it. By contrast, most far right and far left Presbyterians were reared in the church. They stay because they simply have not ever made a choice among denominations. If they did, they might choose a more congenial one.

Church Leaders and Church Staff

As part of my study of the fidelity and chastity debate, I interviewed more than thirty church leaders from across the ideological spectrum and surveyed the General Assembly Council, the denomination's highest enduring representative body. I was looking specifically for the competition among left and right for the center, so this study is most directly on point for our concerns. I asked these church leaders to estimate how most Presbyterian *members* were distributed across the theological spectrum; to estimate how most Presbyterian *leaders* were distributed across the theological spectrum; and to place themselves in the theological spectrum. The results are presented in the table below. I have used the terms that the leaders themselves preferred, noting that baby boomers tend to say "progressive," while other generations say "liberal." All numbers are percentages.

**Figure 6: Distribution of Presbyterian Church (U.S.A.)
across the Theological Spectrum**

	Progressive/ Liberal	Center	Conservative
PC(USA) leaders on members	18	60	23
PC(USA) leaders on leaders	32	50	17
PC(USA) leaders (actual)	27	60	13

All numbers in percent.

One might think that a denominational hierarchy would be in the hands of the denominational loyalists, with the liberals and conservatives exerting pressure from the outside. It is a remarkable fact, though, that informed Presbyterians from across the spectrum believe—even take for granted—that the denominational hierarchy is largely in the hands of liberals, even though the church's membership leans the other way.

How the leadership envisions the distribution of forces in the church affects how they compete within it. In our interviews, the leaders from the different parties were in fairly close agreement that the membership of the church has a few liberals, more conservatives, and mostly centrists. The leaders differed sharply, however, on how skewed they thought the church leadership is. Leaders from the left and center believed that the leadership is twice as liberal as it is conservative, with the remaining majority in the middle. Leaders from the right, by contrast, thought that the leadership is three times as liberal as it is conservative, with only a plurality left in the middle.

In explaining why they thought the left wing was so overrepresented in the church leadership, most respondents suggested that it is simply biased selection by the liberal church establishment, especially from the national headquarters in Louisville, Kentucky. Some liberals I interviewed, though, suggested that liberalism made them more inclusive, and therefore better leaders. One conservative suggested, by contrast, that those who wanted to "renew the church" focused on congregational life, whereas those who wanted the church to "change the world" focused on church headquarters and other denominationwide specialized ministries.

This leads us to findings related to church staff. The Presbyterian Panel includes a group of clergy serving on presbytery, synod, and national church staffs. This group is the most skewed to the left, with a six-to-one Democrat-to-Republican ratio, almost no theological conservatives, and no political conservatives at all. This puts them considerably out of step with the conservative-leaning and predominantly Republican Presbyterian Church. Yet this group also reports the highest rate of valuing their Presbyterian affiliation as part of their Christian identity.

What could account for this? The staff clergy also have a far higher rate of birthright Presbyterians than any other group. This could explain why clergy who are much more liberal than most pastors seem to wind up in the church bureaucracy, rather than moving on to a more liberal denomination.

It is important to note that at the end of the millennium the top leadership of the church took a turn toward the center. In the mid-1990s, when asked if "most of the national leaders of the Presbyterian Church (U.S.A.) seem out of touch with what is happening in local congregations," 57 percent of elders and 64 percent of pastors agreed. When new Stated Clerk Clifton Kirkpatrick and new General Assembly Council Executive Director John Detterick took over at the end of the decade, they attempted to move the church's bureaucracy back toward the center. They aim to reduce the polarizing conflict that threatens the unity of the church. That is also the aim of this book.[5]

Pillars of the Church

We would expect the pillars of the church—its most involved elders and highest status pastors—to reflect this picture of what is normal in the church, only more so. These lay leaders[6] and clergy leaders[7] are at the heart of the loyalist center.

The lay leaders *are* like the regular lay Presbyterians, only more so. Socially, they are almost identical to regular members, differing only in being a bit more educated and a bit less Republican. The real differences show up in their religious life. They take part in worship, congregational volunteering, and Sunday school at much higher rates than do regular members. They pray more, give to the church more, invite friends to worship more, and are more conservative theologically. They are notably stronger when it comes to the Presbyterian Church specifically. They are more likely to have been raised Presbyterian, to have first picked their congregation because it was Presbyterian, to stay because they prefer the Presbyterian Church, to oppose giving church offerings to non-Presbyterian councils, and to say that their affiliation with the Presbyterian Church (U.S.A.) is important to their Christian identity.

The clergy leaders have a notably higher status than the laity, but they agree with their religious views and church practices even more emphatically. Clergy leaders are significantly more likely to be in their first marriages, have advanced degrees, have professional spouses, make high incomes, and live in large cities than are most Presbyterians. They volunteer more in their communities and have notably more Democrats than Republicans, reversing the lay trend. They go to worship and Sunday school even more than the lay leaders, which is not surprising given their jobs, but they also pray, evangelize the unchurched, and give to their congregation at higher rates.

The theological beliefs of Presbyterian clergy leaders are in the same traditional direction as are the lay leaders' but at higher rates, a decisiveness that reflects their longer formal training in theological issues. Clergy leaders show a particularly strong commitment to church life. They almost unanimously reject the view that all religions are equally true, and they rank "religion in my life" slightly ahead of their belief in Christ as their savior. They are the most sympathetic to dissident national church staff, perhaps because they are more likely to know them personally than laypeople are, and they are strongest against putting more emphasis on denomination-dissolving ecumenism. Clergy leaders are the only group to rank creating new congregations as one of their two favorite uses for churchwide offerings, and they strongly embrace the view that their affiliation with the Presbyterian Church (U.S.A.) is an important part of their Christian identity.

Conclusion

What is normal in the Presbyterian Church? To believe that God is and loves us, that Jesus Christ is our savior, that nothing is more important in life than religion. To believe that the Bible shows God's active involvement in all creation, but is not meant to be read as inerrant in each detail. To believe that the gospel is a gift we should bring to the world, not an imposition, because all faiths are not equal, but Christ alone is absolute truth, and God will judge all in the end. To go to church to worship and work, to pray and pay, to be friendly and faithful. And not least, to loyally serve the Presbyterian Church as it is.

If you want to compete and win in the Presbyterian Church, you have to play to what is normal. Play to the pillars, the loyalists. Show them the connection between what you propose and what they already believe and do.

PART III

Where Can We Go?

Introduction

*T*he Presbyterian Church (U.S.A.) is faced with a crisis today that threatens its peace, unity, and purity. The church has been faced with such crises before. At its best, it has weathered these storms by sticking to its constitutional principles. The church has found a way to reach a practical compromise to allow the competition to continue under those constitutional principles.

In this part we will review two great compromises of the past—the Adopting Act of 1729 and the Special Commission of 1925—and look to how the church is seeking the next good compromise through the Theological Task Force of 2001.

In conclusion, I will offer a modest proposal of my own to further the peace, unity, and purity of the Presbyterian Church (U.S.A.).

Chapter 6

Practical Principles for a Competitive Church

*T*he Presbyterian Church is a large, diverse, and complex organization. Therefore, it needs some practical principles to allow it to be both diverse and unified. These practical principles have been developed as compromises in times of crisis. They are principally the work of loyalists trying to hold the church together. Those on both sides who are committed to a pure vision of the church often find these principles unsatisfactory in theory. The church keeps returning to the practical principles, though, because in practice they allow a competition of the opposing extremes while keeping unity, and some measure of peace, in the center.

In this chapter I will lay out three important moments in the search for these practical principles of church competition: (1) the Adopting Act of 1729, with the corollary concerning dissent without schism of 1758; (2) a fuller appreciation of what was said—and was not said—by the Special Commission of 1925, whose work we considered earlier; (3) an initial exploration of the Theological Task Force on Peace, Unity, and Purity of 2001. My concerns here are those of a sociologist, not a historian or constitutional scholar. I will focus on the elements of these famous compromises that affect how the Presbyterian Church holds together as a complex organization and see how they affect the search for a new compromise.

The Good Old Compromise: The Adopting Act of 1729

A crucial debate was held in 1729 between the Philadelphia and New York groups over how strictly ministers should be bound to the Westminster Standards. The Philadelphia group argued for strict subscription to every article. The New York group, by contrast, opposed being bound to any creed, preferring the Bible as the only rule for the church. The Adopting Act of 1729, as it was thereafter known, was the famous and ingenious solution to this problem. Leonard Trinterud, the leading historian of colonial Presbyterianism, estimates that the strict subscriptionists had a two-to-one advantage in the synod meeting, but a compromise was achieved "due to moderates within both parties."[1]

The act declared the Confession of Faith and the Larger and Shorter Catechisms of the Westminster Assembly

> as being, in all the essential and necessary articles, good forms of sound words and systems of Christian doctrine, and [we] do also adopt the said Confession and Catechisms as the confession of our faith. And we do also agree that all the presbyteries within our bounds shall always take care not to admit any candidate for the ministry into the exercise of the sacred function unless he declares his agreement in opinion with all the essential and necessary articles of the said Confession. . . . And in case any minister of this Synod, or any candidate for the ministry, shall have any scruple with respect to any article or articles of said Confession or Catechisms, he shall at the time of his making said declarations declare his sentiments to the presbytery or Synod, who shall, notwithstanding, admit him to the exercise of the ministry within our bounds, . . . if the Synod or presbytery shall judge his scruple or mistake to be only about articles not essential and necessary in doctrine, worship, or government. . . . And the Synod do solemnly agree that none of us will traduce or use any opprobrious term of those that differ from us in these extraessential and not necessary points of doctrine, but treat them with the same friendship, kindness, and brotherly love as if they had not differed from us in such sentiments.[2]

This formula, a potent basis of unity, was put to immediate use. That same afternoon, all the ministers but one, "after proposing all the scruples that any of them had to make against any articles and expressions in the Confession of Faith and the Larger and Shorter Catechisms of the Assembly of Divines at Westminster, have unanimously agreed in the solution of those scruples. . . ." Collectively, they objected to part of the twentieth and twenty-third articles that referred to the role of the civil power in the church and the Protestant succession to the British throne, which they thought inappropriate to American circumstances.[3]

I want to highlight three aspects of this act. The first is the solution to the problem of what ministers had to subscribe to. The strict party wanted Presbyterian ministers to subscribe to the entire Westminster Confession and Catechisms. The loose (or broad church) party wanted Presbyterian ministers, in company with other ministers, to subscribe only to the essential and necessary doctrines of Christianity. The act split the difference: Presbyterian ministers must subscribe to "the essential and necessary articles of the said Confession." This was a loyalist solution because all three parties—strict, broad, and loyalist—could join in adopting it unanimously. Just as important as this formula of "essential and necessary articles" is the fact that the act does not specify which are the essential and necessary articles. Indeed, if the synod could have specified unanimously which were the essential and necessary articles, there would have been no need of the Adopting Act.

This brings us to the second vital loyalist achievement in this act. Any minister who had a "scruple" about any article of the Confession or Catechisms was to explain them to the presbytery or synod (acting, in that case, as a presbytery of the whole). The presbytery was then charged to admit the scrupulous minister unless the presbytery decided that the problem was with an essential and necessary article. This rule entails that there are some nonessential parts of the Westminster Standards, and it presumes that those are what the scruples are likely to be about. About such things reasonable Presbyterians might reasonably differ. We are not told what the individual scruples were on that day, nor how they were resolved. We only know that they were resolved to the satisfaction of the synod. The crucial point for Presbyterian institutional loyalists is that each presbytery makes its own decision about what are essential and necessary articles, within the limits set by the denomination's constitutional confession.

The third element of the act that I want to note is the positive instruction to treat those who disagree with us in the church with friendship, kindness, and brotherly love. If the presbytery admits ministers with whom one disagrees, others in the church are not to undermine their standing in the church or call them nasty partisan names. The tone or institutional culture that loyalists seek to cultivate does not require or expect unanimity. All that is needed is civility and constitutional rule following. Presbyterian loyalists want members of the presbytery to treat one another with decency and orderliness.

Most commentators on the Presbyterian Church treat the Adopting Act as a turning point in the history of the church and a vital part of its living constitution for a long time thereafter. Charles Hodge, probably this country's leading conservative Presbyterian thinker in the nineteenth century, wrote that the Adopting Act "forms an era in our history, and has exerted an influence on our church, which is still felt in all her borders."[4] Charles Briggs, probably our leading liberal Presbyterian thinker at the end of the nineteenth century, wrote:

> Would that the spirit of the Adopting Act had always prevailed in the Church. . . . Would that agreement in the *essential and necessary articles* of the Westminster Standards had ever prevented strife and disunion on

account of differences with respect to unessential and unnecessary articles. This phrase is the pivot of the history of the American Presbyterian Church.[5]

The Adopting Act gives the church a standard of subscription to its essential beliefs that is flexible. A less positive way of seeing the same thing is that the act is ambiguous. This ambiguity gave room for strict and broad subscriptionists to argue competing interpretations for decades, if not centuries. A few years later, in 1736, the synod was asked to clarify whether it had adopted the whole Westminster Confession and Catechisms or not. The synod replied that they did adopt the Westminster Confession and Catechisms, and "we hope and desire that this our Synodical declaration and explication may satisfy all our people as to our firm attachment to our good old received doctrines contained in said Confessions. . . ." This answer was approved by the synod without contradiction.[6]

Charles Hodge believed that this proved the Adopting Act had required strict subscription all along, except for the two articles about the civil power in the church and the Protestant monarchs in Britain that were named in the act. Charles Briggs, by contrast, thought that the original Adopting Act allowed broad and locally flexible subscription, but that this synodical declaration of 1736 tended to replace that broad interpretation with strict subscription.

It seems to me, though, that the words of the 1736 declaration, like those of the 1729 Act, show the same prudent, loyalist flexibility about subscription. The act says that subscription is to the essential and necessary articles of the confession; the declaration says that subscription is to the "good old received doctrines contained in said Confessions." To a loyalist, the great value of the Adopting Act is that it allows the church to hold together while adapting to regional variations. The declaration of 1736 did not undo that flexible adaptation.

The Adopting Act allowed enough room for interpretation that each presbytery could establish somewhat different standards from the others. The strict presbyteries got stricter, and the broad got broader. The Adopting Act required mutual forbearance among ministers whose views differed from one another. When forbearance broke down, these differences sometimes grew into schisms.

In the mid-eighteenth century there was a seventeen-year separation (1741 –1758) between the revivalistic, New York–oriented New Side and the confessional, Philadelphia-based Old Side. When they reunited, they did so on the broad foundation of the Westminster Standards, plus new, postrevival expectations that all ministers had to give evidence of genuine religious experience.[7] Before the separation, when the Old Side were in the majority, they favored strict subscription for all ministers and uniformity among all the presbyteries. After reunion, when they were in the minority, the former Old Side came to see the wisdom of allowing presbyteries to be diverse. In Philadelphia they put up such a fuss about having to examine the religious experience of ministers that a Second Presbytery of Philadelphia, geographically overlapping the First, was erected for them.[8]

The Old Side–New Side reunion of 1758 also introduced an important new standard of civil competition into the Presbyterian Church that remains part of the church's constitution to this day. The Sides separation had been caused by heated invective and illegal exclusions. In order to prevent a repetition of that disaster and to create a form of dissent that would not be considered schismatic, the synod adopted this standard:

> That when any matter is determined by a major vote, every member shall either actively concur with, or passively submit to, such determination; or if his conscience permit him to do neither, he shall, after sufficient liberty modestly to reason and remonstrate, peaceably withdraw from our communion without attempting to make any schism. Provided always, that this shall be understood to extend only to such determinations as the body shall judge indispensable in doctrine and Presbyterian government.[9]

The reference to what "the *body* shall judge indispensable in doctrine and Presbyterian government" (my emphasis) shows the same practical, institution-preserving spirit in the reunion that we saw in the Adopting Act.

At the end of the eighteenth century the Presbyterian Church in the U.S.A. was born with the United States itself, and with parallel forms of balanced government. In 1788 the synod evolved into a General Assembly, and the Westminster Standards were revised and adopted as the constitution of the new church. The ordination vows show the spirit, and some of the language, of the Adopting Act. The first two questions ask ordinands:

1. Do you believe the Scriptures of the Old and New Testaments to be the word of God, the only infallible rule of faith and practice?
2. Do you sincerely receive and adopt the confession of faith of this church, as containing the system of doctrine taught in the Holy Scriptures?

Briggs remarked, "In these ordination vows are wrapt all the principles for which American Presbyterianism had been contending from the beginning— liberal subscription to the *system of doctrine*, a general *approval* of the Presbyterian mode of government and discipline, and the necessity of piety and gracious experience in the ministry."[10]

The practical principles of the Adopting Act were not always adhered to, and the result was schism. At the beginning of the nineteenth century, the revivalistic Cumberland Presbyterians, who did not hold the strict Westminster Confession view of predestination, separated from the rest of the church. In 1837 a separation occurred between the ecumenical, New York–oriented New School and the confessional, Philadelphia-based Old School. By the Civil War, each of these schools had divided into northern and southern churches on questions of slavery, union, and the political role of the church.[11]

The southern Old and New Schools reunited in 1865 to form the Presbyterian Church in the United States (PCUS), and the two schools united in the north in 1870 to form the Presbyterian Church in the United States of America (PCUSA). The southern and northern churches remained apart until 1983. While parallel developments were occurring in both denominations, the more dramatic struggles occurred in the northern branch.[12]

During this separation Princeton Seminary became the leading intellectual institution of the Old School, and Union Seminary in New York become the leading intellectual institution of the New School. Princeton was directly controlled by the denomination, while Union was formally independent but effectively Presbyterian. With the reunion of the two schools in the north in 1870, each side recognized the orthodoxy of the other, and the Westminster Confession was retained in the constitution of the new church, with the Adopting Act as the standard of subscription. In the reunited church, Philadelphia and Princeton remained conservative centers, while New York and Union provided leading liberals. The leading moderates generally were found outside the northeastern base of the two extreme parties.[13]

In 1967 the northern Presbyterian Church wrote a new confession. The church also adopted a new theory of the place of confession in the constitution. Rather than substituting the Confession of 1967 for the Westminster Standards, the church created a *Book of Confessions*. Since the Adopting Act referred specifically to the Westminster Confession and Catechisms, the act could no longer be the constitutional standard for subscription to the confession.

The spirit of the Adopting Act lived on, at least for a time. It could be revived.

The Good New Compromise: The Special Commission of 1925

In adopting the report of the Special Commission of 1925 without debate, the General Assembly united around a centrist compromise very much like that of 1729. They settled on three points that all have resonance for today: (1) that no governing body of the church can, by itself, declare essential doctrine; (2) that tolerating difference in nonessential doctrine is a basic constitutional principle of the church; and (3) that church officers have a right to the freedom of conscience that protects dissent, but not defiance and schism.

In the dispute between the five fundamentals and the Auburn Affirmation, the Special Commission articulated a centrist position. They also agreed with the conservatives on the five fundamentals as true doctrines of the Presbyterian Church. And they agreed with the liberals that those five fundamental doctrines, and the theories proposed to explain them, could not be established by the General Assembly as doctrinal tests. But the larger point, they said, was that essential doctrines could be established by the church at any time, *if* constitutional procedures were followed. The General Assembly cannot amend the constitution by itself. The constitution can be amended, however, by the General Assembly with the concurrence of the presbyteries.

The General Assembly's adoption of the Special Commission report is still being misinterpreted. The Assembly's conclusion that it could not change the constitution of the church to define "essential and necessary articles" without the concurrence of the presbyteries is taken by some to mean that the church thinks it cannot change its constitution *at all*. This is like saying that since Congress cannot amend the United States Constitution without the concurrence of the states, the Constitution cannot be amended at all—a similarity not at all coincidental as the constitutions of both church and state were created together.[14]

The report of the Special Commission of 1925 articulated the principle, quoted earlier, that "toleration when rightly conceived and frankly and fairly applied is as truly a part of our constitution as are any of the doctrines stated in that instrument." This is another way of saying the essential point of the Adopting Act. The report goes on beyond the language of church constitutional law to talk about the culture of the church. The report continues:

> Presbyterianism is a great body of belief, but it is more than a belief; it is also a tradition, a controlling sentiment. The ties which bind us to it are not of the mind only; they are ties of the heart as well. There are people who, despite variant opinions, can never be at home in any other communion. They were born into the Presbyterian Church. They love its name, its order and its great distinctive teachings. In its fellowship they have a precious inheritance from their forbears. Their hearts bow at its altars and cherish a just pride in its noble history. Attitudes and sentiments like these are treasures which should not be undervalued hastily nor cast aside lightly. A sound policy of constitutional toleration is designed to conserve such assets

whenever it is possible to do so without endangering the basic positions of the Church.[15]

The Special Commission's idea of toleration in nonessentials is rooted in a very loyalist vision of the Presbyterian Church as a great institution, as our institution. In contrast with the too-inclusive liberals, "they love its name, its order and its great distinctive teachings." Against the too-pure conservatives, they articulate this principle of *constitutional* toleration in nonessentials, and the sociological notion that "Presbyterianism is a great body of belief, but it is more than a belief." The Presbyterian Church is not just a peculiar historical byway waiting to rejoin the church in general; neither is it just an association of individuals who happen to read the Bible the same way. The loyalist sees the church as a particularly valuable organic institution, constituted by its whole constitution. "Attitudes and sentiments like these are treasures which should not be undervalued hastily nor cast aside lightly."

Just as the Adopting Act of 1729 had its corollary about legitimate dissent in 1758, so the Special Commission of 1925 had its corollary about legitimate dissent in a report adopted by the General Assembly in 1934. In that year the General Council, the executive body of the General Assembly, responded to several overtures about the Independent Board of Presbyterian Foreign Missions with "Studies in the Constitution of the Presbyterian Church in the U.S.A." This was the basis of the Council's recommendation, subsequently adopted by the full General Assembly, that all officers of the Presbyterian Church resign from the Independent Board.

After detailing the history of its efforts to deal with Machen's charges, the "Studies" offered a careful argument about how an agency like the Independent Board should be treated under the constitution of the Presbyterian Church. It stated that the church (as, ironically, Machen himself had argued) is a strictly voluntary body, but when one volunteers to join it, one accepts certain rules and principles given by its constitution. All officers of the church voluntarily vow to promote the peace and unity of the body.[16]

The church's constitution has explicit protections for the expression of conscience or private judgment, which were acknowledged and asserted in the "Studies." This question of "private judgment" had, however, been something of a problem, as some minorities in the church had tried to use this protection to justify ignoring the judgments of the church courts and circumventing the agencies of the church. In the Presbyterian Church, the "Studies" maintained, the "right of private judgment has always been 'unalienable.'" However, "an individual cannot claim the right to two opposite private judgments at one and the same time. In the Presbyterian Church the assumption of office is an exercise of private judgment." This concept of "two opposite private judgments" was then developed this way:

> If, however, during the course of his tenure of office the time comes when he insists that according to his present private judgment he no longer approves the government and discipline of the Presbyterian Church, . . . then he is exercising an entirely different private judgment from that which he originally exercised when inducted into office. . . . No constitutional Church could exist by allowing one private judgment which professed approval to the government and discipline of the Church, and at the same time admitted another contrary private judgment which renounced the rule and authority of the Church. A Presbyterian office holder, therefore, . . . must either submit to the provisions as established in the Constitution in the Church, or declaring that his conscience no longer will allow him to submit himself to the Church which has the rule over him, renounce the advantages which the Presbyterian Church bestows upon all who sincerely receive and adopt her distinctive principles, and withdraw from his office. God is a God of order, not confusion, in the Presbyterian Church in the United States of America.[17]

This argument reasserted the traditional policy of the Presbyterian Church on questions of conscience. This tradition was a generous policy when compared with the absolute claims of some churches in the past, for it struck a balance between the integrity of the individual conscience and the need for order and unity in the organized church. Particularly relevant in Machen's case was the provision that one could in conscience withdraw from the church without being considered a schismatic, *if* one did not try to make a schism. The Assembly made its argument on the assumption that anyone who opposed the General Assembly and its judgments would not wish to be in the Presbyterian Church.

At the time of the Special Commission of 1925, the Presbyterian Church commonly looked for leadership from its tall-steeple pastors and its elders who had responsible public roles. The Special Commissioners were all older white men, nearly all of them married fathers. By today's standards they were not a diverse group. By the standards of 1925, though, they had the kind of diversity that the church valued most, balanced by a common practical experience of church life. They were diverse, first, according to the bedrock structural principle of Presbyterianism; namely, they had a balance of ministers and elders. Second, they were diverse geographically, drawn from the several synods of the church.

The Special Commission was unmistakably drawn from the heart of the

Presbyterian Establishment. They all had shown a long commitment to the practical institutions that make up the daily life of the Presbyterian Church: its schools, its committees, and, most important, its congregations. To read even their thumbnail sketches is to see a church that honored its leaders, a church that *had* an Establishment from whom it could draw in times of crisis. At that time, the Presbyterian Church—in common with most American institutions—understood the sociological value of giving honor or "status" to those most committed, most loyal, to the institution itself.

The members of the Special Commission of 1925 were the following:

Henry Swearingen, the chairman, who was 56 when the Commission was formed, and had been pastor of the House of Hope Presbyterian Church in St. Paul, Minnesota, for eighteen years. A Pennsylvanian, he had graduated from Westminster College and Allegheny Theological Seminary, both institutions of the United Presbyterian Church in his native state. For many years he served as a trustee of Macalester College and of McCormick Theological Seminary (then called the Presbyterian Theological Seminary of Chicago), both PCUSA schools. He was deeply involved in the Presbyterian Church in the U.S.A., serving as Moderator of the Synod of Minnesota, President of the Presbyterian Home Mission Council, and on the Executive Committee of the Presbyterian Alliance. Swearingen was also involved in Presbyterian cooperation with other churches, serving in the denomination's Department of Church Cooperation and Union, as a delegate to the Pan-Presbyterian Council and to the Universal Conference on Life and Work, and on the Executive Committee of the Federal Council of Churches.

Mark A. Matthews, 58, was pastor of the largest church in the denomination, First Presbyterian of Seattle, which had some eight thousand members. Born into an active Presbyterian family in Georgia just after the Civil War, Matthews had no schooling beyond the middle of high school. He read heavily, especially in the theology of Princeton Seminary professor Charles Hodge, and was licensed to preach as a teenager. He threw himself into reform work, especially against alcohol, and while a pastor in Tennessee taught himself law and passed the bar to help the reform cause. From Tennessee he was called to Seattle, where he was a combative reformer and a very successful church builder. Though he often attacked "modernism" in the Presbyterian Church he was also committed to its institutions, serving as a trustee of Whitworth and Whitman Colleges and of San Francisco Theological Seminary.

Hugh T. Kerr, 54, had been pastor of Shadyside Presbyterian Church in Pittsburgh for twelve years. A Canadian, he had studied at the University of Toronto before enrolling in Western Theological Seminary, a PCUSA school in Pennsylvania. Before his pastorate he taught at McCormick Seminary. His son and namesake would later be a well-known Princeton Seminary professor, and another son would be a Presbyterian minister. Kerr was President of the denomination's Board of Christian Education at the time of the Special Commission, and he would later head the Western Hemisphere section of the (World) Alliance of Presbyterian and Reformed Churches.

Lapsley McAfee, 61, was in the middle of a twenty-five-year pastorate at First Presbyterian Church in Berkeley, California. Son of the founder of (Presbyterian) Park College in Missouri, McAfee was of a family well-connected in the Presbyterian Church for generations. A strong supporter of Asian missions, he died in the Philippines in 1935 while inspecting institutions formed by missionaries sent by his congregation.

Harry Clayton Rogers, 48, had been the very successful pastor of Linwood Boulevard Presbyterian Church in Kansas City for seventeen years. Reared in a strong Presbyterian family in Kentucky, he attended the church's Centre College, of which he was later offered the presidency, and McCormick Seminary, of which he became a trustee. He was also a trustee of Park and Lindenwood Colleges. He served for many years on the General Council of the PCUSA, including thirty years on its evangelism committee.

Two other loyalist pastors, less prominent than those above, were **Alfred H. Bar**r, 57, of Chicago after long pastorates in Detroit and Baltimore, and **Edgar W. Work**, 64, once pastor of what became Lapsley McAfee's congregation in Berkeley, later of New York City.

A strong figure on this commission, and chairman of the 1926 General Assembly commission that investigated Princeton Seminary was **William Oxley Thompson**, 70, then completing twenty-six years as president of Ohio State University. A graduate of the church's Muskingum College and Western Theological Seminary, Thompson regarded himself as a preacher who happened to be a college president. He was chairman of the Board of Trustees of the (Presbyterian) College of Wooster, trustee president of the Westminster Foundation, and for forty years a trustee of Lane Theological Seminary. He was President of the International Sunday School Union in 1918, Moderator of the Synod of Ohio in 1925, served on the General Council, budget committee, and Department of Church Cooperation and Union of the PCUSA, and at the time of his death in 1934 was a member of the Joint Committee on Organic Union with the United Presbyterian Church of North America.

Of the seven lay ruling elders, six were eminent men in secular institutions, and the seventh was a prominent bureaucrat of the Presbyterian Church. They were:

John M. T. Finney, 62, vice-chairman, a surgeon at Johns Hopkins Hospital in Baltimore. The grandson, son, and brother of Presbyterian ministers in Maryland (his father was a graduate of Princeton Seminary), Finney graduated from Princeton University and Harvard Medical School. He was an elder of the Brown Memorial Church in Baltimore, where J. Ross Stevenson had been pastor before assuming the presidency of Princeton Seminary. One of the most eminent doctors in the country, he had been President of the American Surgical Association, the American College of Surgeons, and of the Southern Surgical and Gynecological Association, and had been offered the presidency of Princeton University after Woodrow Wilson's resignation. Finney was a trustee of Princeton Seminary during the conflict later in the 1920s, and served as Vice-Moderator of the General Assembly under his college classmate Charles Erdman.

John H. DeWitt had just been appointed a Judge of the Tennessee Court of Appeals in 1925 at the age of 53. The son of a prominent Presbyterian minister, he attended Vanderbilt University and Columbia College of Law (in Washington D.C.), and was an elder of Hillsboro Presbyterian Church in Nashville for thirty years. DeWitt was President of the Tennessee Historical Association, and served as Chairman of the Judicial Commission of the Presbyterian Church in 1923.

Cheesman A. Herrick, 57, had been President of Girard College in Philadelphia for fifteen years in 1925. A graduate of the Wharton School of the University of Pennsylvania, from which he received a Ph.D., Herrick had served the Presbyterian Church as an elder of Arch Street Presbyterian Church in Philadelphia, as a member of the Board of Foreign Missions, and as Vice-Moderator of the General Assembly.

The other three secular professionals played a less prominent role in the church, if not in the world. **Nelson Loomis**, the General Solicitor of the Union Pacific Railroad in Omaha, had served the church's New Era Movement and the Layman's Council. **Edward Duffield** was the President of the Prudential Insurance Company. **Nathan Moore**, who descended from a long line of Presbyterian ministers in Pennsylvania and served as elder and organist in his own church, was a prominent Chicago attorney.

Robert Speer was the most eminent churchman among the ruling elders on the commission. At 57, Speer was in the middle of a forty-year term as the Secretary of the church's Board of Foreign Missions. The son of a Pennsylvania Congressman, Speer was raised in a deeply Presbyterian home. After graduating from Andover he went to Princeton University, where he was a leader of the Young Men's Christian Association and the missionary Student Volunteer Movement, as well as a varsity athlete, editor of the college newspaper, and valedictorian. He attended Princeton Seminary, leaving before graduation to work for the Board of Foreign Missions, but returned years later as President of the Board of Trustees of Princeton Seminary, where the library is now named for him. Speer was also President of the Federal Council of Churches.

The final participant in the work of the Special Commission of 1925 was its secretary, Stated Clerk **Lewis Mudge**. At 60, Mudge was completing the first of three five-year terms as the elected administrator of the denomination. Descended from a long line of ministers, he attended Princeton University, and at Princeton Seminary he roomed with Robert Speer. He was pastor of Pine Street Presbyterian Church in Harrisburg, Pennsylvania, when first elected Stated Clerk in 1921. A trustee of (Presbyterian) Wilson College and Princeton Seminary, he was elected Moderator in 1931.

The commission was decidedly moderate-to-conservative theologically, and one member, Mark Matthews was a noted fundamentalist. In fact, Erdman later credited Matthews with first proposing the commission at the 1925 General Assembly. The weight of the commission lay with men who were successful in the pastorate or in the secular professions. Few were academics, few were known for their religious polemics, and none were of the liberal party in the church.

The most striking indication of the centrality of this group of loyalists to the Presbyterian Church is the extraordinary line of Moderators of the General Assembly it contained. The moderatorship is the highest honor and most powerful and symbolic office in the church, and moderatorial elections were seriously contested between conservatives and loyalists from the 1910s through the 1930s. Mark Matthews, the most conservative member of the commission, was elected Moderator in 1912, and chairman Henry Swearingen won in 1921. Charles Erdman, who appointed the commission, was elected with loyalist and liberal votes in 1925. He was succeeded by William O. Thompson in 1926, the year the commission made its initial report, and by Robert Speer in 1927, the year of the group's final report. Cleland McAfee, brother of commission member Lapsley McAfee, was elected in 1929, Hugh Kerr in 1930, Lewis Mudge in 1931 (concurrent with his reelection to a third five-year term as Stated Clerk), and Harry Clayton Rogers was a candidate for the moderatorship in 1932. In addition, Elders John Finney and Cheesman Herrick each served as Vice-Moderators.

Looking for the Next Good Compromise: The Theological Task Force on Peace, Unity, and Purity of 2001

Today we are faced with a sustained crisis in the Presbyterian Church like that of the 1920s. Progressives and evangelicals send competing overtures to the

General Assembly nearly every year. As soon as the Assembly ends, the "judicial season" begins, as closely watched cases make their way through the church courts. There is talk of schism and invitations to the other side to "take a hike."[18] Most presbytery executives have publicly called for a "third way" between left and right.[19] And the center of the church is sick to death of the annual battles.

In response, the 2001 General Assembly created the Theological Task Force on the Peace, Unity, and Purity of the Church to deal with the contested issues before the church, as well as their underlying causes. The task force is explicitly modeled on the Special Commission of 1925.

The immediate run-up to the 2001 General Assembly in Louisville had several challenges to the peace, unity, and purity of the church. In addition to the long-running competition over fidelity and chastity, detailed above, there was the dust-up both over remarks at a Peacemaking conference and over the more consequential Confessing Church Movement.

In July 2000, Rev. Dirk Ficca asked the Presbyterian Peacemaking Conference, "What's the big deal about Jesus?" Ficca, a Presbyterian minister and executive director of the Council for a Parliament of the World's Religions, urged Christians to abandon their "instrumental" view of salvation, which holds that "salvation comes solely through Jesus . . . that Jesus himself is the Good News . . . (and) that the goal of the Christian faith is the establishment of Christendom."[20] In response to conservative requests for an official repudiation of these views, the General Assembly Council issued a response that appeared to conservatives to be equivocal. The Council later admitted that its response was inadequate.[21]

The Confessing Church Movement was born out of conservative frustration with the denomination's apparent ambiguity about some central doctrines. Inspired by the Ficca case and the fidelity and chastity issue, several churches issued their own confessions. The Presbyterian Lay Committee took up the movement and spread it nationwide. All the various versions of this confession agree that Jesus Christ is the sole way to salvation; that Holy Scripture is infallible; and that marriage between a man and a woman is the only appropriate context for sexual activity. Ten to 15 percent of the denomination's congregations signed on.[22]

The 2000 General Assembly was faced with an overture from Beaver Butler Presbytery in Pennsylvania declaring that there was an "irreconcilable impasse" in the church. The Assembly overwhelmingly rejected this overture, 453 to 71 (86 percent to 14 percent).[23] Instead of promoting division, the Assembly had elected Rev. Syngman Rhee as Moderator on a platform of reconciliation.[24] Rhee spent his moderatorial year traveling the church, promoting reconciliation and seeing the divisions firsthand.

Just before the 2001 General Assembly, Rhee issued a statement calling for a theological commission. He wrote:

> In looking forward to the 213th General Assembly, I have looked back to other times in the life of our denomination when disagreements and conflicts seemed ready to tear our church asunder. I note especially the 1925 General Assembly wherein a special commission was appointed "to consider the spiritual condition of the church and to make . . . proposals which may promote purity, unity, peace, and progress." . . . Perhaps it is time once again to establish a "commission" to help us in seeking this more excellent way, a way guided by the Spirit of Christ seeking mutual understanding and enabling us to speak the truth in love.[25]

John Calvin Presbytery in Missouri sent an overture calling for such a commission to the 2001 General Assembly. The church's three top officials—Rhee, Stated Clerk Clifton Kirkpatrick, and General Assembly Council Executive Director John Detterick—all testified in favor of the proposed commission.[26]

The 2001 General Assembly voted to create a Theological Task Force on Peace, Unity, and Purity by a vote of 467 to 41 (92 percent to 8 percent). The main charge to the task force is "to lead the Presbyterian Church (U.S.A.) in spiritual discernment of our Christian identity in and for the 21st century, seeking the peace, unity, and purity of the church." The Assembly created a task force, rather than a commission, because the constitution requires a commission to be composed of ministers and elders, and the Assembly wanted the task force to be able to include some practicing homosexuals who were barred from serving as church officers. The task force would be named by the Moderators of the 1999, 2000, and 2001 General Assemblies (that is, Freda Gardner, Syngman Rhee, and Jack Rogers) and was to report to the 2005 General Assembly. It was to be composed of seventeen members "reflecting the theological and cultural diversity of the Presbyterian Church (U.S.A.)." Elder Jenny Stoner, who chaired the committee that proposed the task force to the whole Assembly, would later be named co-moderator of the task force.[27]

In October 2001 the Moderators announced that, of some 500 nominations, they had chosen twenty-one persons for the task force. They had expanded the number set by the Assembly "in order to represent adequately the strengths and diversity needed." The individuals were commended to the church not because they represented various constituencies, but on the loyalist grounds that they "represent the heart of this great church." The task force was charged to confer widely in the church on matters that unite and divide Presbyterians, including, "issues of Christology, biblical authority and interpretation, ordination standards, and power." In the end, the task force "may recommend ways by which we can live more faithfully together in the 21st century."[28]

The task force was composed as follows, listing ministers and then elders:[29]

Co-moderator **Gary W. Demarest** is a longtime pastor. From 1988 to 1993 he served as Associate Director of Evangelism and Church Development for the Presbyterian Church. When the task force was named he was the interim pastor of the 1500-member Glenkirk Presbyterian Church in Glendora, California.

Elizabeth R. Achtemeier was a retired adjunct professor of Bible and Homiletics at Union Theological Seminary in Virginia. She died a year into the taskforce's work.

Milton J Coalter is Professor of Bibliography and Research and directs library and information technology services at Louisville Presbyterian Theological Seminary. He was co-editor of the seven-volume Presbyterian Presence series.

Victoria G. Curtiss is Co-Pastor of Collegiate Presbyterian Church in Ames, Iowa. She was formerly the Executive Presbyter in Western Reserve Presbytery in Ohio.

Frances Taylor Gench is Professor of New Testament at Union Theological Seminary and Presbyterian School of Christian Education.

Jack Haberer is Pastor/Head of Staff of Clear Lake Presbyterian Church in Houston, Texas.

William Stacy Johnson is the Arthur M. Adams Associate Professor of Systematic Theology at Princeton Theological Seminary.

Jong Hyeong Lee is Pastor/Head of Staff of Hanmee Presbyterian Church, Itasca, Illinois, and former professor of church history at Presbyterian Theological Seminary, Seoul, Korea.

John B. (Mike) Loudon is the Pastor/Head of Staff of First Presbyterian Church of Lakeland, Florida.

Lonnie J. Oliver is Pastor/Head of Staff of New Life Presbyterian Church in Atlanta and adjunct professor of Evangelism and Missiology at Johnson C. Smith Seminary/Interdenominational Theological Center.

Martha D. Sadongei is part-time stated supply serving Central Presbyterian Church, Phoenix, and an enrolled member of the Kiowa tribe of Oklahoma.

Sarah Grace Sanderson (later **Sanderson-Doughty**) was a student at McCormick Theological Seminary when named to the task force. During the course of its work she became pastor of the Presbyterian Church in Lowville, New York.

José Luis Torres-Milán is Pastor/Head of Staff of Tercera Iglesia Presbiteriana (Third Presbyterian Church) in Aguadilla, Puerto Rico.

John Wilkinson is Pastor of the Third Presbyterian Church of Rochester, New York.

Co-moderator **Jean S. (Jenny) Stoner**, retired Director of the United Way of Kentucky, was also formerly Interim Coordinator of the Office of Global Education and International Leadership Development, Worldwide Ministries Division, PC(USA). Now living in East Craftsbury, Vermont, she chaired the General Assembly committee that proposed the task force.

Scott D. Anderson is Executive Director of the California Council of Churches.

Barbara Everitt Bryant is a Research Scientist, University of Michigan Business School, and from 1989 to 1993 was Director of the U.S. Bureau of the Census.

Mary Ellen Lawson is the Stated Clerk and Associate for Administration in Redstone Presbytery in Pennsylvania.

Sue Mallory is the Executive Director of Leadership Training Network and the founding Director of the office of Lay Ministries at Brentwood Presbyterian Church. She withdrew from the task force for health reasons at the outset.

Joan Kelley Merritt, a former high school science teacher, is Moderator of the Presbytery of Seattle.

Barbara G. Wheeler is President of Auburn Theological Seminary and Director of Auburn's Center for the Study of Theological Education.

Staffing the task force is **Gradye Parsons**, Associate Stated Clerk of the Presbyterian Church (U.S.A.).

At their first meeting in December 2001 in Dallas, the task force developed a covenant to govern their work that pledged them to consensus procedure whenever possible. They divided into four working groups to consider scriptural and theological resources; historical and ecclesiastical resources; practices that are conducive to discernment and community-building, including models from the mission field; and consultation and communication with the larger church.[30]

When we examined the thumbnail sketches of the members of the Special Commission of 1925, we found the heart of the Presbyterian Establishment: pastors and elders, married white men, who had devoted themselves to the institutions of the Presbyterian Church in the U.S.A. Of the eight ministers, seven were tall-steeple pastors and one was a university president. Of the seven elders, six were leaders in the secular professions and one was a church bureaucrat. Most important, none of them had been significant players in the fundamentalist-modernist competition within the national church.

The Task Force of 2001 seems to have been constructed on a different principle. They were not drawn from the heart of the Establishment—if we can even still speak of a Presbyterian Establishment—but to "represent the heart of this great church." Many of the members of the task force were publicly identified with one side or another of the church's ideological competition. In fact, many of them seem to me to be in an ideologically balanced pairing with another task force member. Moreover, the task force is quite diverse in sex, age, region, and racial ethnic composition. The task force is so diverse, in fact, that the only thing they all have in common is the church.[31]

Since this was a task force and not a commission, the body was not obliged to be balanced between clergy and elders. Of the twenty-one members initially chosen, thirteen were clergy and eight were elders. Scott Anderson, a former minister who resigned his office when he came out as a gay man, had been ordained a youth elder in the early 1970s and installed by his local session a few years before the task force was created. Sarah Sanderson, was, at the time of her appointment, an elder and a senior at McCormick Seminary, but was ordained and installed as a pastor in the first year of the task force's work. Another elder, Sue Mallory, had to resign for health reasons before the task force began its work, and was not replaced. So, by the end of the task force's first year of work, it had 14 ministers and six elders.

The task force had a balance of men and women, as well as considerable racial ethnic diversity. This is a bedrock structural principle in Presbyterian bodies today. The group initially had eleven women and ten men, which became an even split after the resignation of Sue Mallory. In racial ethnic terms, the task force included one African American, one Puerto Rican, one Native American, and one Korean American, and seventeen Anglos of various European backgrounds.

Occupationally, pastors were the largest single group, with nine (or ten, counting Sanderson)—nearly half the body. In this the task force resembles the Special Commission. The Special Commission pastors were drawn from the larger churches of the denomination, whereas the task force pastors come from a much more varied group of congregations. They range in size from the 1,500-member churches served by Gary Demarest and Mike Loudon, to the 60-member church where Martha Sadongei is stated supply preacher.

Among the elders, the difference between the Special Commission and the task force is more striking. The 1925 elders were prominent men in the world, as well as long-term church volunteers: a leading doctor, a major corporation president, an appellate judge, two prominent lawyers, a college president, and one church bureaucrat. On the task force the six remaining elders are a professor (and former Director of the Census Bureau), a retired schoolteacher, a retired United Way director and sometime denominational official, and three church professionals: a seminary president, a state Council of Churches director, and a presbytery stated clerk.

What strikes me most about the vocations of the task force as compared to the Special Commission is the predominance of seminary professors. On the Special Commission, there were none. On the task force, there is one seminary president, four seminary professors, two adjunct seminary professors—and for good measure, a seminary student.

Finally, whereas the Special Commission avoided the recognized leaders of the competing ideological groups of the day, the task force is marked with such leaders. The chair, Gary Demarest, is a well-known "open" or embracing evangelical, brought in to head the denomination's evangelism office in the early days of the reunited church bureaucracy. The co-moderator, Jenny Stoner, a United Way director and professional volunteer, is also a former denominational official, and her husband is the former top program bureaucrat, General Assembly Council Executive Director S. David Stoner. Both Stoners have, in my judgment, a moderately liberal reputation.

The best-known women on the task force, former Union Seminary (Richmond, Virginia) professor Betty Achtemeier and Auburn Seminary president Barbara Wheeler, are among the foremost intellectual disputants in the church on the right and left, respectively. Jack Haberer was moderator of the conservative Presbyterian Coalition during the fidelity and chastity contest, while Scott Anderson was co-moderator of Presbyterians for Lesbian and Gay Concerns at that time. Mike Loudon is pastor of a conservative Confessing Church Movement church, while John Wilkinson is pastor of a liberal More Light church and on the executive board of the liberal Covenant Network. William Stacy Johnson, while not clearly identified with either side in the several recent controversies, had taken positions on most of them in his column in the *Presbyterian Outlook*. Not all the participants, to be sure, are as easily identified as leaning one way or the other. But clearly, the task force was composed with ideological balance in mind, whereas the Special Commission was composed almost entirely of unaffiliated institutional centrists.

After the death of Elizabeth Achtemeir in 2002, she was replaced by her son, Dubuque Seminary professor Mark Achtemeir. He represents a theologial position similar to his mother's.

Although most of the task force members are identifiable with a distinctive ideological position, they seem to have been chosen because they are people capable of crossing lines to reach out to the other side.[32]

The task force also differs notably from the Special Commission of 1925 in the way it set about its work. The Special Commission briskly divided up their task, took testimony from various members of the church in one meeting, produced draft reports, and then presented a preliminary report to the General Assembly in one year. They took another year to perfect their report, but its essentials were created in their discussions with one another in a few meetings. The task force, by contrast, set out allowing much more time for the process of communication with one another and with the church. Their initial four-year mandate was extended to five (2006) by the shift of General Assemblies to biennial sessions. The emphasis on process reflected, in part, the much greater ideological diversity of the new as compared with the old church committee.

The task force met with focus groups of commissioners to the 2002 General Assembly. They identified the central themes of these focus groups thus:

> There is consensus that we [Presbyterians] agree upon far more issues than we disagree upon. *We have got to find ways to agree to disagree and to respect each other[s] differences.*[33]

The Theological Task Force on Peace, Unity, and Purity of 2001 is set on the road to find the next good compromise for the Presbyterian Church.

Chapter 7

A Modest Proposal: Presbyters Rule!

*M*y central proposal for strengthening the loyalist center of the Presbyterian Church is this:

> Make the constitution real.
> Let the presbyteries decide.
> Let the presbyters rule.

Make the Constitution Real

The loyalists are the great constituency of the constitution in the church. They are the pillars who hold up both parts of the constitution: order and confession. It has been difficult, however, to be loyal to the confession lately because the Presbyterian Church does not have a confession; it has many. Which means, in effect, that it has none.

The confessions are subordinate to Scripture, which is subordinate to Jesus Christ. A confession has always been an important part of the church's constitution, though, because the church needs an authoritative institutional standard for how it is to interpret Scripture as the witness to Jesus Christ.

I have not talked very explicitly about the *Book of Confessions* or its place in the church that loyalists are loyal to. In effect, though, I have been talking all along about the importance of having a confession, having a clear theological standard, having a real church for the pillars to uphold. The issue in the Adopting Act of 1729 was how strictly officers had to subscribe to the Westminster Confession, the confession that constituted the theological interpretation of Scripture for the Presbyterian Church. The issue for the Special Commission of 1925 was what part of the church could decide which articles of the confession were necessary and essential for officers to accept. Both compromises, and all the great struggles of the Presbyterian Church since its founding, have turned on how the church's confession was to regulate the faith and manners of presbyters. As the *Book of Order* says, through the confessions the church declares to itself and to the world "who and what it is, what it believes, what it resolves to do."[1] The confession does, indeed, matter.

So what happened? The *Book of Confessions* happened. In 1958 the Presbyterian Church in the U.S.A. (northern Presbyterians) merged with the United Presbyterian Church of North America. A committee was created to come up with a brief statement of faith for the new United Presbyterian Church in the U.S.A. Princeton Seminary professor Edward Dowey chaired the committee, and his theory of confessions changed the direction of the committee's work, and then changed the church in a profound way. The committee, after several extensions and changes of mission, did write a new document. It was not just a brief statement of faith, but a medium-sized confession organized around the theme of reconciliation. The Confession of 1967 had a number of important theological innovations, and it spurred a number of conservative protest groups, the most enduring of which is the Presbyterian Lay Committee.

More important than what the confession itself said was the proposal that came with it to create a whole book of confessions. Professor Dowey, an expert on confessions, argued that confessions should not be seen as permanent statements of the truth, but rather were produced by a particular part of the church at a particular time responding to particular circumstances. Indeed, they deliberately called their work the Confession of 1967 to emphasize its temporal—and temporary—nature. C67 was to be a useful statement for the church at that moment. And by the same token, the Westminster Confession, which had served as the constitution of the church for two centuries, was really just a statement from its time. The church would not be bound in the future by what it said in 1967, so why should it be bound by what it had confessed in the 1630s, even if it had reiterated that confession in the 1730s and 1830s and 1930s? In fact, the church had produced all sorts of useful creeds, from the earliest days right up to living memory. Why not, they argued, declare a whole set of them to be equally the "confessions" of the church?[2]

Thus was born the *Book of Confessions*. It consisted, initially, of the Nicene Creed, the Apostles' Creed, the Scots Confession, the Heidelberg Catechism, the Second Helvetic Confession, the Westminster Confession of Faith, the Westminster Shorter Catechism (the Westminster Larger Catechism was dropped, but later restored at reunion), the Theological Declaration of Barmen, and the Confession of 1967. As a result of the 1983 reunion of the northern and southern Presbyterian Churches, the new Presbyterian Church

(U.S.A.) later added A Brief Statement of Faith. This *Book of Confessions* officially constitutes Part I of *The Constitution of the Presbyterian Church (U.S.A.),* followed by Part II, the *Book of Order.*

Professor Dowey was no doubt correct that it is valuable academically to see confessions as documents of a particular moment in the church. Institutionally, however, they can function quite differently. The Westminster Confession was not a dead document of the past, but a living part of the constitution of the Presbyterian Church. The Presbyterian Church could know what it believes because it was constituted by what it confessed.

Consider this comparison. The Presbyterian Church in the (new) United States of America adopted a constitution in the 1780s that included the Westminster Confession and catechisms. The (new) United States of America adopted a constitution in the 1780s, too. Both institutions grew and developed for almost two centuries, *constituted*, in part, by their constitutions. From time to time both church and nation amended their constitution, with the central legislature proposing amendments and supermajorities of its constituent bodies (presbyteries, states) deciding whether to adopt them or not. In the 1960s, both constitutions faced severe challenges, especially on the issue of race. The United States rose to the challenge and made laws that lived up to its creed. The Presbyterian Church, by contrast, did not face these new challenges within its constitution, but instead added a variety of other constitutions, including a new one that finally finished off the fight that had already been settled by the Special Commission of 1925.

This analogy is not perfect. The U.S. Constitution resembles the *Book of Order*, while the Westminster Confession is analogous to the Declaration of Independence. But the church, unlike the state, is explicitly confessional. The Presbyterian Church was, and still is, officially constituted by its confession as well as by its order.

Dowey admitted that the point of proposing a book of confessions was to eliminate the authority of Westminster, or any confession, to set bounds to the faith and manners of church officers. The committee that produced the *Book of Confessions* had the high-minded purpose of saving the church from legalism and scholasticism, of remaining open to the Holy Spirit. As Professor Douglas Ottati of Union Seminary in Virginia wrote, in celebration of C67 and the *Book of Confessions*, ". . . the point of confessions is not to mandate or constrain a detailed agreement. Neither is it simply to frame a more general consensus. The point of confessions is also to spur and sustain an ongoing theological conversation within a living tradition."[3] Yet the institutional effect of the *Book of Confessions* was something different. Compare this "theological conversation" standard with the standard set in the Adopting Act:

"And we do also agree that all the presbyteries within our bounds shall always take care not to admit any candidate for the ministry into the exercise of the sacred function unless he declares his agreement in opinion with all the essential and necessary articles of the said Confession."[4]

The *Book of Confessions*, in my opinion, removed the Adopting Act from the constitution of the Presbyterian Church.

Furthermore, compare the theory of the *Book of Confessions* with the third constitutional question, or ordination vow, asked of all officers of the church today:

Do you sincerely receive and adopt the essential tenets of the Reformed faith as expressed in the confessions of our church as authentic and reliable expositions of what Scripture leads us to believe and do, and will you be instructed and led by those confessions as you lead the people of God?[5]

The ordination vow that we use today, quoted here, reflects the southern Presbyterian tradition, and was adopted by the whole church in the reunion of 1983. It has a stronger role for the confessions than did the looser, northern vow of Dowey's day.[6] It seems to me that there is simply a contradiction between our vow to receive the essential tenets of the Reformed faith from the confessions, and the reality of a book that is not taken to be essential or necessary in its real role in the constitution.

The *Book of Confessions* has made all the confessions apocrypha—useful for individual edification and devotion, but not constitutive of the church.

Let me offer several kinds of evidence to support this conclusion. First, the precipitous decline in Presbyterian Church membership began at about the time of the Confession of 1967. Several causes started this decline, but one factor often cited in explaining why it continues is the difficulty the Presbyterians have in evangelizing, in answering the question, "What does your church believe and why should I believe it?" When the church stopped being constituted by a clear confession, it became much harder for ordinary loyal Presbyterians to explain what the Presbyterian Church believes—to themselves as well as to others.

As a second small bit of evidence, let me cite my own experience in serving on a task force on family life of the national church. I had thought that the material in the confessions on marriage and raising children would form much of the starting point of our discussion of family life. In the end, however, a majority of the skilled, competent, and, I think, representative ministers and elders on the task force concluded that what the confessions said about family life were statements of their time, but had no compelling authority for the church today. The *Book of Confessions* was only meant for "guidance." This is somewhat different, it seems to me, from being "instructed and led by those confessions."

Third, I asked a representative sample of Presbyterian clergy, "If the *Book of Confessions* were ever revised, which ones would you personally definitely want to keep?" The table below shows the results.

Figure 7: Presbyterian Ministers' Assessment of the Confessions

Confession	Percent to keep Pastors	Percent to keep Spec. Clergy	Percent to keep Conservative	Percent to keep Center	Percent to keep Liberal
Nicene	70	66	85	76	78
Apostles'	73	69	85	82	84
Scots	49	38	56	53	59
Heidelberg	51	46	67	56	57
Second Helvetic	44	38	51	48	60
Westminster	63	58	81	67	73
Shorter Catechism	62	57	81	64	73
Larger Catechism	54	51	70	57	63
Barmen	64	57	71	71	84
C67	60	52	52	68	87
Brief Statement of Faith	63	48	54	73	87

All numbers in percent.

If it were up to the church's clergy, few of our confessions would be adopted by the required supermajority. Stated Clerk Clifton Kirkpatrick, the church's chief diplomat and leading optimist, and his coauthor William Hopper assert that the Presbyterian Church, "with 'one heart and one voice' turn, further, to our confessions for doctrinal guidance."[7] I truly wish it were so, but I do not believe that the evidence bears them out.

The theory of the *Book of Confessions* rests on a sociological misunderstanding that we have encountered often in these pages. The Presbyterian Church is an institution. It is not simply an aggregation of individuals who happen to share beliefs in common, or, more to the point, *don't* share beliefs in common. It is certainly not just a society for the academic study of what Presbyterians in the past have believed. The church as a living institution needs a substantive standard of what it believes and is trying to do. The church needs an authoritative standard of what it confesses, so that it can know what its mission is, and have some guidance about how to do it. The church also needs a clear and authoritative theological constitution so that, to draw on one of Calvin's distinctive marks of a true church, it can discipline those who stray from that authoritative standard. The *Book of Order* says, "The church is prepared to counsel with or even to discipline one ordained who seriously rejects the faith expressed in the confessions."[8] To do that, however, we have to seriously *believe* the faith expressed in the confessions.

The absence of a true confession for the church has created a vacuum. Into this vacuum has been pushed the *Book of Order.* Since the creation of the *Book of Confessions*, the action in the church, both in the General Assembly and in the church courts, has shifted to interpretation of the only part of the constitution with practical significance in the institutional functioning of the church, the *Book of Order.* The *Book of Order* has also, not coincidentally, gotten much longer and more specific as a result. The theological vacuum has been so great that the theological bits of the *Book of Order* itself have been pressed into service as a de facto theological standard for the church. The Great Ends of the Church, articulated in the *Book of Order*, G-1.0200, have been lifted up for general guidance and study by the church, most notably in an abortive effort to make them the theme of six successive General Assemblies.

It will not be easy to rebuild an authoritative, constitutional confession for the church. Since the '60s, authority of all sorts has been in a bad odor in the Presbyterian Church. Personal experience, not theological understanding, are what we lift up as authoritative for many church decisions. The institutional church was seen as deadly to the Holy Spirit, and putting fetters on prophets. It is surely true that the presence of the Spirit is absolutely vital to the church. Sheer institutional loyalty can never be the sole standard of faith and practice.

A full theology of the church is beyond what sociology, or this sociologist, can offer.[9]

Nevertheless, the church is a real institution. It needs theological boundaries as much as it needs boundaries of orderly process and physical walls. Without a real and full theological constitution, the presbyteries will have no firm boundaries to their decisions, and the presbyters will have no clear standards by which to rule. Respecting authority does not prevent competition, as we saw in the struggles of the 1920s; it just makes it possible to settle them.

Recent developments have given the church an unexpected motivation to take the confessions more seriously. The fidelity and chastity amendment, G-6.0106b of the *Book of Order*, has two clauses. The first concerns, naturally, fidelity and chastity. The second, though, gives a new seriousness to the confessions as an active part of the constitution. The second clause reads: "Persons refusing to repent of any self-acknowledged practice which the

Confessions call sin shall not be ordained and/or installed as deacons, elders, or ministers of the Word and Sacrament." The silver lining of the fidelity and chastity storm could be that we finally must take seriously—in fact, we must find out, as a church, for the first time—what it is that the confessions call sin.

Let me clear up a couple of possible misunderstandings of my point here. First, I am not specifying *how* the church should make its confession real, make it a living part of its constitution again. I am not suggesting that we simply restore the Westminster Standards. We could make each potential officer of the church go systematically through the *Book of Confessions*, affirming or explaining scruples about each point, and then offering a personal harmony of the whole. We could take some of the confessions—say, the Apostles' Creed, the Nicene Creed, the Barmen Declaration, the Westminster Confession, and the Brief Statement of Faith, to take those with the greatest pastoral support—and officially harmonize them. We could write a new, comprehensive confession. We could do a number of other things. But we must do something to make it possible for our ordination vows to be meaningful.

The most promising proposal that I have seen thus far is Stated Clerk Clifton Kirkpatrick's call for a missional constitution. He proposes taking the first four chapters of the *Book of Order* as the starting point for a leaner constitution for the Presbyterian Church (U.S.A.). As I envision such a project, the mission of the church would then be determined in various ways by the subsidiary governing bodies of the church, its sessions and presbyteries, under the general guidance of the essential doctrines and broad principles of order set by the constitution.[10]

Which brings me to a second possible misunderstanding. I am not suggesting that each officer of the church must subscribe to every article of the confession or confessions. That issue was well settled by the Adopting Act. It is the task of the ordaining body—presbyteries in the case of clergy, sessions in the case of elders—to seriously consider whether officers of the church sincerely subscribe to the essential and necessary articles of our confession.

This, in turn, brings me to my second major proposal.

Let the Presbyteries Decide

The presbytery is the basic constituent institution of the Presbyterian Church. As the "reserve clause" of our constitution reads,

> The jurisdiction of each governing body is limited by the express provisions of the Constitution, with powers not mentioned being reserved to the pres-

byteries, and with the acts of each subject to review by the next higher governing body.[11]

Kirkpatrick and Hopper, commenting on this basic principle, conclude that "[o]ur church was organized from the bottom up, so the powers given to the General Assembly by the presbyteries were only those specifically named."[12] I would put it that the Presbyterian Church was organized from the center out—from the presbytery.

It has long been true that the presbytery was the basic institutional unit of the Presbyterian Church, and this fact is deep in our church's culture. William Chapman, in his survey of the *Book of Order* with the wonderful subtitle, "Blood on Every Page," notes that it was actually the Special Commission of 1925 that formally articulated this idea of the original and reserved powers of the presbytery. In fact, this theory was not officially made part of the constitution of the church until 1994.[13] The church has not yet fully absorbed the implications of this constitutional principle.

The principle that the presbytery is the basic constituent institution of the Presbyterian Church leads me to support local option in deciding ordination standards, that is, local option, *within* the boundaries of the constitution. The Adopting Act said that officers of the church must subscribe to the essential and necessary articles of our confession. It wisely did not specify those necessary and essential articles, but left it to each presbytery (or in the case of elders, each session) to decide. The presbytery starts with the presumption that each potential officer of the church is in full agreement with the Presbyterian constitution; it then hears the scruples of each candidate and decides on a case-by-case basis. The constitution of the whole church is honored, and the individuality of each officer is humanely considered.

Local option does not mean that every candidate gets ordained. Sometimes the just thing for the presbytery or session to do is to say no. Moreover, just because a person is ordained in one presbytery does not mean that he or she will be automatically admitted to "labor within the bounds" of another. Ordination is for the whole church, but where one can practice specific ministries is up to the presbytery. This requires that the Presbyterian Church go back to the old practice of each presbytery seriously examining candidates for the ministry as well as ministers wishing to transfer or work within the presbytery. Moreover, presbyters are supposed to voluntarily bring their scruples back to the presbytery if they change their minds about any aspect of the confessions. The presbyteries and sessions have to be serious and tough-minded about their oversight of the church, and especially of other presbyters. In the words of Rev. Vic Pentz, who succeeded the late Frank Harrington, Senior

Pastor of Peachtree Presbyterian Church in Atlanta, "going back to our fore-bears might be the key to success for our church. . . . What if we became less easy to please, more feisty?"[14]

Local option would not require, and need not promote, nongeographic presbyteries, such as the old, overlapping First and Second Philadelphia Pres-byteries of the eighteenth century. The geographic presbyteries we have now are already theologically diverse. Keeping geographic presbyteries will help moderate the competition.

I do not believe that the presbyterian polity is the only legitimate Christian polity, and neither does the church. I do, however, believe that there is great sociological wisdom in our "middle way" organization. The wisdom of pres-byterian organization is most apparent when we try to deal with theological diversity in the church. Every complex institution has diversity in it. Local option lets the strict presbyteries be strict and the loose presbyteries be loose, while all stay within the bounds set by the constitution. That is the traditional Presbyterian way of living with diversity. The problem of strict or loose sub-scription to the confessions has always been with us in the church, and it will be until Jesus comes. The solution we keep coming back to is local option under the constitution.

If local option is the traditional solution, what is the problem? The prob-lem is that whenever one wing or the other has a temporary majority in the General Assembly it tends to try to impose its position on the whole church. The conservatives tried to do that with the five fundamentals. They were dealt with by the Special Commission of 1925. The liberals did that with women's ordination. Today, when the issue is homosexual ordination, many of the lib-erals wish they had not succeeded so well in suppressing local option. And now it is the turn of the conservatives to try to impose a churchwide standard on *that* hotly contested issue.

The current problem with local option goes back to the Kenyon case. Wal-ter Wynn Kenyon was a candidate for ordination in Pittsburgh Presbytery in 1974. He had a scruple about participating in the ordination of a woman, yet he would accept women's ordination and work with them if they were ordained by others. The presbytery determined that this scruple did not vio-late any essential and necessary article of the confessions, and would be an acceptable accommodation of the church's order. The ordination was appealed, though. Ultimately the General Assembly Permanent Judicial Com-mission determined that the presbytery had erred, that Kenyon did propose to violate an essential and necessary article of Presbyterian faith, and therefore that he could not be ordained.[15] Presbyteries did not have a local option in deciding about who would participate in ordaining women.

Following up on their victory in the Kenyon case, liberals at the 1978 UPCUSA General Assembly proposed a controversial overture to require that every congregation have women, as well as men, as deacons and elders. The first vote in the Assembly was tied, 276 to 276. On a second consideration the proposal passed by just six votes. The measure then went to the presbyteries as Amendment L. It passed by a vote of 79 presbyteries to 70, and became part of the church's constitution.[16]

Amendment L is a good example of what the Special Commission of 1925 established. And this is a good place to emphasize, one last time, what the commission really said, because this important point is still being misunderstood. The commission did *not* say that the General Assembly could not determine what are necessary and essential articles of faith for presbyters. What it did say was that the General Assembly *acting alone* could not determine necessary and essential articles. In fact, no governing body in the church *acting alone* can determine essential and necessary articles. What was wrong with the five fundamentals was not that the General Assembly proclaimed them, but that the Assembly never sent them down to the presbyteries for ratification. In the case of Amendment L, by contrast, the amendment to the constitution was sent down to the presbyteries, and it was ratified by a majority of them. The amendment won, fair and square, and is part of the constitution (G-14.0201). Just as fidelity and chastity is (G-6.0106b).

Winning a competition, however, is not like winning a war. In a competition, you still have to live with your competitors, who will come back again next year. The year of Amendment L, 1978, was also the year of definitive guidance in the homosexual ordination struggle. In the Kenyon case and Amendment L, liberals undermined the principle of local option on which the Adopting Act depended. Now, especially after their loss in the most recent Amendment A vote, liberals wish they had a form of local option again. Their victory was constitutional, but imprudent. In fact, some liberals have inquired whether there is any way to apologize to Walter Kenyon, without actually changing the result of his case.[17] The wisdom of the Adopting Act keeps coming back to the surface, no matter how many times the church pushes it under.

For presbyteries to really be decisive, they need strong presbyters, which brings me to my third proposal.

Let the Presbyters Rule

The pillars of the church are the presbyters. The *Book of Order* says, "This church shall be governed by presbyters (elders and ministers of the Word and

Sacrament, traditionally called ruling and teaching elders)" (G-4.0301b). To be sure, there are many, many loyal members who carry on the faith and ministry of the church in their daily lives and their own vocations. Still, the institution of the church is held up, in the main, by the teaching and ruling elders, the presbyters. When officers of the church are installed in a congregation, the congregation is asked, "Do we agree to encourage them, to respect their decisions and follow as they guide us, serving Jesus Christ, who alone is Head of the Church?" In a minor miracle of collective understanding, and without consulting with one another, the congregation answers on one another's behalf, "We do."[18]

Vic Pentz said, in the speech quoted above, that the church needs to "return leadership to its best leaders: elders." You will probably not be surprised to learn that I, a ruling elder of the church, find this argument from a leading pastor of the church heartwarming. It is a natural tendency for a church to let its clergy run things, especially the clergy in the church bureaucracy. Ruling elders need to step up to their vocation again and again, to fulfill their duty to the church. And the church, in turn, should build up the body of elders who are most devoted to the church itself. These are the true pillars around which every level and body of the church can be built.

The other body of presbyters who have been undervalued in the church of late are the tall-steeple pastors. In 1925 the Presbyterian Church had an informal Establishment of leading pastors that it could draw on who could be depended on to be respected by the church and astute about its institutions. Since the cultural revolution of the 1960s the Presbyterian Church has systematically undermined the Establishment that it had, and most especially of anything that might look like a "good old boys network" of leading pastors. Yet this has not had the effect of democratizing the church. It has simply shifted leadership away from those who successfully run the church's most complex grassroots institutions, its large churches, and created a new elite of denomination-level bureaucrats. It will be difficult to get tall-steeple pastors to take a more active role in the committees and offices of the church, as they are already nearly consumed by very demanding, and more rewarding, congregational work. The only coin that the church could pay that could make that sacrifice worthwhile is the coin of honor, status, or prestige in the church, and some measure of authority.

The lay leaders and pastoral leaders of the church are the natural pillars of this or any denomination. If we want to strengthen the loyalist center of the Presbyterian Church, we need to consciously build up their stability and respect in running the larger institutions of the denomination.

While we are strengthening the natural pillars of the church, we should also, I believe, end the well-intentioned but misguided antiestablishment experiments with youth elders and nonpresbyter advisory delegates. Elders are elders for a reason, reflecting long and deep sociological wisdom in the church. It makes a great deal of sense for the church to invest significantly in leadership development among youth and theological students. However, the role of Youth Advisory Delegates at the General Assembly, has been, in my estimation, a disaster.

Ecumenical advisers, as elders of other churches, are a different matter altogether. If I had my druthers, the General Assembly would have as its advisory delegates the two groups with the most thorough knowledge of the church's constituent presbyteries: the executive presbyters, and that most "decently and in order" group in the church, the stated clerks.

Two groups that need to step back a bit from leadership in the church are specialized clergy and professors. The specialized clergy, as we have seen, are the least representative group in the church, yet are disproportionately— sometimes dominantly—the leaders of the church's controversies. In some presbyteries large numbers of specialized clergy do not participate at all in presbytery life, yet show up to vote on controversial issues. To be sure, specialized clergy perform many valuable ministries for the church as a whole. Their voice should be heard in the councils of the church. But I believe that it would be prudent if the predominant weight in running the church were given to those responsible for the day-to-day life of the congregations.

About professors, well, let me, a professor, quote Rodney Stark and Roger Finke, two other professors, about the usual effect of professors on church life: "[I]ndeed, it was in the religion departments and divinity schools, not in the science departments, that unbelief was formulated and promulgated in American intellectual life."[19] I am not suggesting anything like a purge, but much greater forbearance.[20]

The Dialogue about Competition and Conflict in the Church

As I noted at the outset of this book, I am making an argument here in dialogue (and also, it must be said, in competition) with the arguments put forth by four significant leaders of the Presbyterian Church (U.S.A.). I would like to close by briefly comparing my arguments with theirs.

Clifton Kirkpatrick and William Hopper Jr., make a strong case for *What Unites Presbyterians*. I largely agree with them, and have cited them several times. Kirkpatrick and Hopper are loyalists, trying to strengthen the center.

They emphasize that the several groups in the Presbyterian Church (U.S.A.) have much common ground on which to build. I believe that the Stated Clerk, by his own inclination and by the structural demands of his position, is an optimist and a promoter of agreement. I honor this disposition and largely share it. I do think, though, that there are serious differences between the liberal and conservative wings of the church on the authority of Scripture, on the authority of the confessions, and on authority in general. These differences will continue to divide them for the foreseeable future. They, in turn, will compete to convince the center of the church to follow them. This competition will not end.

Jack Rogers, former Moderator and longtime laborer, in *Claiming the Center* of the church, argues that the main division in the church is between a liberal leadership and a conservative membership. "The congregational side," he writes, "emphasizes the need to ground people in the biblical and confessional tradition. The governing body side," by contrast, "stresses the need to enable people to cope creatively with modernity."[21] His argument is that the church needs a balance of both sides. The Task Force of 2001, which he had a significant role in choosing, shows this idea of balance. He also believes that both sides have the same underlying Christian worldview, but that it has been overlaid with political ideologies that drive them apart. I agree that both sides that he describes are in the church and will remain so for a long time, so a balance between them is better than having one or the other dominate, especially at the governing body level.

Rogers says the liberal leadership got there in a way that subverted what I would call the pillars of the church. He writes:

> In their eagerness to accomplish an agenda of inclusivism, the liberal leadership of the Presbyterian and other mainline churches subverted their own rules of representative government. So-called elected leaders fill positions on our national councils and committees and task forces but were never elected. Generally they get these positions by being screened through a national nominating process. That process is built on the liberal worldview that the primary requisite for any church entity is being as inclusive as possible. As a result we get people in places of leadership who have not come up through the ranks. They have never been elected by anyone in a local congregation to any office. They are good people, but they are not a representative of the church but rather of some special interest that someone on a nominating committee thought should be highlighted.
>
> I am not arguing that we should be less inclusive. I am pleading that we be authentically inclusive.[22]

This is in line with what I have been arguing, stated even more strongly. My only difference here with Jack Rogers is that I do not see in his work thus far any mechanism that would accomplish that authentic inclusivity. Constitutional competition could accomplish it. Ironically, in naming the Task Force of 2001, Rogers was obliged to use the same process he here criticizes.

I am in strong agreement with Jack Haberer's argument in *GodViews*. He sees the church divided, not into a three-part competition of the left and right for the center, but into five GodViews, or Christian worldviews, each of which is needed in the church. He likes the loyalist theory, but says, humorously, that "[w]hile many centrist moderates are out there somewhere, at last count the number of truly loyal Presbyterians had dropped to about seventeen (okay, I'm exaggerating a little bit)."[23] His central category, the Ecclesiasts, resemble the loyalists in many ways, and Haberer allows that most Presbyterians fall into this category. The image that he proposes for how we deal with the competition of GodViews in the church is to have an immense number of café tables in the Astrodome. At each table would be five chairs, one each for the Confessionalist, Devotionalist, Ecclesiast, Altruist, and Activist GodViews, and let them talk out church conflicts over an open Bible.

I part company with Jack Haberer only at the end, at this image. I believe that he is speaking of, and to, only the leaders of the various factions in the church. His image of the conversations at the café tables makes most sense if we are thinking of committed members of articulate GodViews. The loyalists that I have in mind are rarely that articulate about one vision of the church or another, even the Ecclesiast view, though they would probably resonate to it the most. They don't have a theory of the church; they just do it.

My second point of disagreement is one that has come up often in this book. The kind of face-to-face dialogue (or pentalogue, if there is such a word) that Haberer envisions is not on the scale of institutional competition in a national denomination like the Presbyterian Church (U.S.A.). Even if you had a whole Astrodome full of tables, we could not bring the whole church together, or even all the informed and concerned members of the church together. In the actual competitions in the church, the leaders of the GodView parties are not really talking to one another—they are competing for the church masses who are not attached to any organized GodView. They are just loyal to the church.

Constitutional competition has worked for the Presbyterian Church before. Even in a time such as this, when the peace, unity, and purity of the church are threatened as they have not been in three generations, the church can find the new good compromise—like the old good compromises—that will let us have competition within our constitution again.

Here is what I think of as the Loyalist Text from the *Book of Order*:

The Presbyterian system of government calls for continuity with and faithfulness to the heritage which lies behind the contemporary church. It calls equally for openness and faithfulness to the renewing activity of the God of history. (G-4.0303)

PART IV   Appendix

Figure 8: The Three Presbyterian Parties in the Early Twentieth Century

Strongest in	Conservatives	Loyalists	Liberals
Presbytery	Philadelphia	—	New York
Seminary	Princeton	McCormick	Union in New York
Leaders	J. Gresham Machen, Princeton Seminary Professor	J. Ross Stevenson, Princeton Seminary President	Henry Sloane Coffin, Union Seminary President
	Clarence Macartney, Pastor	Charles Erdman, Princeton Seminary Professor	Robert H. Nichols, Auburn Seminary President
	Mark Matthews, Pastor	Robert Speer, Foreign Mission Secretary	Henry Van Dyke, Princeton University Professor
	Maitland Alexander, Pastor		
	David Kennedy, *Presbyterian* editor		

Figure 9: Parties in the Fidelity and Chastity Competition

Left	Center	Right
Presbyterians for Lesbian and Gay Concerns	**Former Moderators**	**Presbyterian Lay Committee**
Scott Anderson	Bob Bohl	Warren Reding
Laurene LaFontaine	John Buchanan	Parker Williamson
Jane Spahr	Marj Carpenter	**Genevans**
Witherspoon Society	Price Gwynn	Jerry Andrews
Jeff Doane	Clinton Marsh	Bill Giles
David McGowan	Harriet Nelson	Al Ruth
Eugene TeSelle	**Presbyterian Center**	David Snellgrove
Bruce Tischler	**(headquarters) Staff**	Robert Taylor
Former Moderators	John Burgess	**Presbyterians for Renewal**
John Fife	Frank Diaz	Betty Moore
Herbert Valentine	Cliff Kirkpatrick	Joe Rightmyer
Presbyterian Center	Joe Small	**Presbyterians Pro-Life**
(headquarters) Staff	**Pastors**	Terry Schlossberg
James Brown	Joanna Adams	**Presbyterians for Democracy**
Vernon Broyles	Craig Barnes	**and Religious Freedom**
Curtis Kearns	**Academics**	Alan Wisdom
Mary Ann Lundy	John Mulder	**Former Moderators**
Belle Miller McMaster	Jack Rogers	David Dobler
Eunice Poethig	Jack Stotts	**Pastors**
Mark Wendorf	Louis Weeks	Clayton Bell
Pastors	**Editor**	Howard Edington
Eugene Bay	Robert Bullock	Jack Haberer
Norm Pott		Frank Harrington
Gail Ricciuti		Harry Hassall
Academics		Roberta Hestenes
Cynthia Campbell		John Huffman
Jane Dempsey Douglas		John Stevens
Hugh Halverstadt		Walter Ungerer
Douglas Ottati		**Academics**
Barbara Wheeler		Dale Brunner
Writers		Darryl Fisher Ogden
John Frye		Tom Gillespie
Chris Glasser		Darryl Guder
		Stacy Johnson
		Brad Longfield
		Don McCollough
		Bruce McCormick
		Terry Muck
		Andrew Purvis

This table represents the common answers of a group of church leaders from across the spectrum whom I surveyed in 1996 and 1997, during the "fidelity and chastity" amendment vote. They were asked to name leaders in the Presbyterian Church at the left, center, and right. Those listed were *not* asked to verify their placement.

Figure 10: Presbyterian Seminary Alumni, 1990

Variable Name	Most Alumni	Liberal Alumni N=502	Middle Alumni N=583	Conservative Alumni N=385	Denomination Staff N=40
Baby boomer (aged 31–45)	64	67	68	74	50
B average college grades[1]	57	52	57	71	58
Own income $25K or more	60	55	62	68	78
Male	65	48	70	87	45
Married/Divorced (N, not percent)	78/6	70/9	80/5	89/1	55/25
Went to southern seminaries[2]	49	42	53	50	43
Pastor now	70	61	72	83	NA
Medium city or smaller	64	58	66	70	44
Congregation of 260 or fewer	51	42	50	65	68
A parent is a college graduate	69	64	53	51	57
Nonscience college major	60	61	61	53	50
From UPCUSA[3]	55	58	55	50	64
Ordained minister	85	83	85	92	78
Firmly for local ministry	46	30	51	60	15
Bible in historical context[4]	47	77	38	9	72
God transcendent and immanent[5]	81	72	88	65	87
Strong for denominations[6]	52	51	57	29	58
Theological middle[7]	59	NA	NA	NA	60[8]
Support two or more children	47	41	49	56	33
Live in the South	42	37	41	37	47
Started seminary "middle of the road" theologically[9]	40	41	43	18	45
Finished seminary "middle of the road" theologically[10]	42	21	55	28	35

Total number of respondents (N) = 1390
All numbers in percent.

Figure 11: Presbyterian Students
at Presbyterian and Non-Presbyterian Seminaries, 1990

Variable Name	All N= 893 (349)	Liberal N= 235 (76)	Middle N= 537 (207)	Conservative N= 102 (58)
Male	64 (52)	51 (28)	67 (46)	82 (78)
Bible in historical context[11]	68 (59)	94 (95)	65 (57)	18 (18)
God transcendent and immanent[12]	82 (81)	76 (82)	89 (84)	64 (69)
Started seminary "middle of the road" theologically[13]	40 (23)	27 (16)	49 (77)	17 (8)
Finished seminary "middle of the road" theologically[14]	39 (18)	17 (5)	51(26)	61 (4)
In the M.Div. program	56 (79)	* (80)	* (79)	* (85)
Want to be pastor in ten years[15]	53 (38)	* (61)	* (37)	* (13)[16]
Attended a private college	57 (56)	* (71)	* (52)	* (50)
From the South	23 (22)	* (21)	* (21)	* (25)
Big on church as child	60 (46)	* (*)	* (*)	* (*)
From medium city or smaller	47 (43)	* (*)	* (*)	* (*)
Congregation of 500 or fewer	50 (40)	* (*)	* (*)	* (*)
A parent is a college graduate	66 (66)	* (*)	* (*)	* (*)
Nonscience college major	70 (67)	* (*)	* (*)	* (*)
B average college grades	60 (58)	* (*)	* (*)	* (*)
From UPCUSA[17]	64 (61)	* (*)	* (*)	* (*)
Gen X (under 30)	29 (35)	* (*)	* (*)	* (*)
Married/Divorced	67/7 (60/6)	* (*)	* (*)	* (*)
Support two or more children	23 (22)	* (*)	* (*)	* (*)
In a southern seminary[18]	40 (NA)	* (*)	* (*)	* (*)
Intend to be ordained	86 (74)	* (*)	* (*)	* (*)
Strong for denominations[19]	52 (34)	* (*)	* (*)	* (*)
Theological middle[20]	62 (61)[21]	* (*)	* (*)	* (*)

Key = Presbyterian Seminaries (Non-Presbyterian Seminaries)
Total number of respondents (N) = 893 (349)
All numbers in percent.
* = No significant differences among liberal/middle/conservative.

Figure 12: The Presbyterian Panel, 1994–96

Variable (All responses in percent)	Lay Member	Lay Leader	Clergy Leader	Far Right[22] N=124	Far Left[23] N=166	Staff Clergy[24] N=56
Age 40-64	59	53	81	52	68	84
First marriage	70	70	83	70	58	64
Two or three kids	64	57	68	59	59	48
College graduates +	59	67	+52[25]	48	84	+30[26]
Professional or executive	58	63	—	52	77	—
Spouse professional or executive	58	56	83	49	68	87
Income $50K +	49	52	88	54	73	56
Medium city or smaller	57	61	40	61	48	42
Know most neighbors	70	70	NA[27]	74	65	NA
Community volunteer	69	68	89	72	79	79
Republicans/Democrats	55/25	50/31	32/45	80/11	7/73	11/67
Political extremes/moderates	5/48	3/44	7/53	52/3	35/18	20/38[28]
Raised Presbyterian	41	44	44	53	51	77
Came for Presbyterian Church	34	38	NA	38	24	NA
Join for friendliness/sermons	17, 17	22, 14[29]	NA	20, 15[30]	17, 15	NA
Stay for spirit/Presbyness	63, 36	63, 38	NA	68, 58[31]	55, 48[32]	NA
At worship nearly weekly +	74	95	96	80	69	91
Spend much other time at church, too	65	96	NA	71	63	NA
Invite two + friends yearly	66	70	52[33]	66	52	18[34]
Give 5% + of income	52	66	83	79	48	83
Sunday school nearly weekly	52	78	84	80	57	48
Volunteer in congregation	76	94	78	81	75	86
Pray for guidance weekly +	66	86	93	86	72	92
Theological extremes/moderate	9/52	8/46	7/51	—	—	18/52
Their faith most important	57	65	86	67	58	84
Top belief: God loves me	73	84	90	92	67	86
Second: Christ is savior	61	78	66[35]	84	57[36]	59[37]
Bible not inerrant in details	59	57	88	15	92	98
Bible shows God in creation	79	84	90	62	92	96
Reject "only those in church will be saved"	66	54	74	12	96	91
Accept "God will judge all"	59	65	64	89	20	56
Reject "all religions true"	71	80	95	82	56	93
Accept "Christ is the only truth"	64	70	72	94	19	57
Evangelizing isn't imposing	71	73	75	89	26	65
Better society from converts	74	75	66	64	63	61
Presbyterian is important to Christian identity	64	73	82	66	86	89
Give for relief/poor needs	24, 15	21, 16	27, 16[38]	21, 18	17, 13	15, 21
Not for church council/environment	33, 20	38, 26	37, 15[39]	26, 19	36, 19[40]	39, 24[41]
Hold Headquarters staff accountable	84	84	74	80	76	79
Don't ordain homosexuals	65	68	61	58	54	55
Do attend to member loss	78	83	78	88	78	95
Don't chase ecumenism	69	53	80	88	71	76
Do promote biblical faith	53	56	67	63	62	68
Don't chase social issues	52	58	68	72	58	58

Notes

FOREWORD

1. William J. Weston, *Presbyterian Pluralism: Competition in a Protestant House* (Knoxville: University of Tennessee Press, 1997).

INTRODUCTION: THE COMPETITIVE CONSTITUTIONAL CHURCH

1. Evan Silverstein, "Most clergy expect split in PC(USA), survey finds," *Presbyterian News Service #01296*, August 24, 2001. According to the Presbyterian Panel, the church's ongoing survey of members and officers, a majority of elders, and almost three quarters of pastors, thought a large schism somewhat likely by 2050.

2. Jack Rogers, *Claiming the Center: Churches and Conflicting Worldviews* (Louisville, Ky.: Westminster John Knox Press, 1995); Jack Haberer, *GodViews: The Convictions That Drive Us and Divide Us* (Louisville, Ky.: Geneva Press, 2001); Clifton Kirkpatrick and William H. Hopper Jr., *What Unites Presbyterians: Common Ground for Troubled Times* (Louisville, Ky.: Geneva Press, 1997).

3. I am grateful to Ron Afzal for this point.

4. I am grateful to Mark Tammen for this point.

5. See Louis Weeks and William J. Fogelman, "A 'Two-Church' Hypothesis," *Presbyterian Outlook*, 172, no. 12 (March 26, 1990): 8–10.

INTRODUCTION TO PART I

1. Lefferts A. Loetscher, *A Brief History of the Presbyterians,* Fourth Edition (Philadelphia: Westminster Press, 1983), 61–77.

2. Leonard J. Trinterud, *The Forming of an American Tradition: A Re-examination of Colonial Presbyterianism* (Philadelphia: Westminster Press, 1949).

3. Part I is a condensed version of a story I tell in much greater detail in *Presbyterian Pluralism: Competition in a Protestant House* (Knoxville: University of Tennessee Press, 1997).

CHAPTER 1. TOO BIG: THE INCLUSIVE LIBERAL CHURCH OF CHARLES A. BRIGGS

1. Lefferts A. Loetscher, *The Broadening Church: A Study of Theological Issues in the Presbyterian Church since 1869* (Philadelphia: University of Pennsylvania Press, 1954), 42; Channing Renwick Jeschke, "The Briggs Case: The Focus of a Study in Nineteenth Century Presbyterian History" (Ph.D. diss., Divinity School, University of Chicago, 1966), 286–87;

Francis Patton, in *New York Times,* "Articles of Faith" (1893); *New York Sun,* "The New Reformation" (1889), n.p.; see also Philip Schaff, in *New York Tribune* (1889), n.p. For Briggs's later assessment, see Charles A. Briggs, "Note Biographical, 1841–1889" (April 1, 1889, typescript; in Briggs Papers, Union Theological Seminary, Box 44, Folder 33), 1; Charles A. Briggs, *The Defense of Professor Briggs before the Presbytery of New York, 1893* (New York: Charles Scribner's Sons, 1893), 88; Charles A. Briggs, "The Future of Presbyterianism in the United States of America," *North American Review* (July 1893; in Briggs Papers, Union Theological Seminary, Box 52, Folder 28), n.p.; Max Gray Rogers, "Charles Augustus Briggs: Conservative Heretic" (Ph.D. diss., Columbia University, 1964), 382.

2. Mark Massa, "Charles Augustus Briggs and the Crisis of Historical Criticism" (Th.D. diss., Harvard Divinity School, 1987), 48; Jeschke, "Briggs Case," 104, 139; Carl Hatch, *The Charles A. Briggs Heresy Trial: Prologue to Twentieth Century Liberal Protestanism* (New York: Exposition Press, 1969), 23.

3. Charles A. Briggs, *American Presbyterianism: Its Origin and Early History* (New York: Charles Scribner's Sons, 1885), 140, also xii–xiii; idem,*Whither?: A Theological Question for the Times* (New York: Charles Scribner's Sons, 1889), 88; idem, "The Future of Presbyterianism in the United States of America," n.p.

4. Charles A. Briggs, Letter to Francis Brown, November 8, 1888, quoted in M. G. Rogers, "Briggs: Conservative Heretic," 81.

5. Charles A. Briggs, "Union of Northern and Southern Presbyterians," 1888, n.p. He makes specific reference to the Woodrow case, in which a southern seminary professor was treated unjustly, according to Briggs and many northern critics, for his "advanced" views on evolution.

6. Briggs, *Defense of Professor Briggs, 1893,* 17.

7. Charles A. Briggs, *The Ethical Teachings of Jesus* (New York: Charles Scribner's Sons, 1904), 50–51.

8. *Biblical Study,* 1883, 36–37; quoted in William R. Hutchison, *The Modernist Impulse in American Protestantism* (Cambridge: Harvard University Press, 1976), 92.

9. Briggs,*Whither?,* 16–17.

10. Ibid., 247–48.

11. Briggs, "The Alienation of Church and People," 1893, 74.

12. Charles A. Briggs, "The Advance Toward Church Unity," in *The Independent* (January 1, 1891; in Briggs Papers, Union Theological Seminary, Box 52, Folder 1), 1.

13. Robert Wuthnow, *The Restructuring of American Religion* (Princeton, N.J.: Princeton University Press, 1988).

14. Charles A. Briggs, *The Authority of Holy Scripture: An Inaugural Address* (New York: Charles Scribner's Sons, 1891; reprint New York: Arno Press, 1972), 33–35, 43–45.

15. It was later charged that the conservatives pushed this motion through the presbytery meeting while the Union Seminary people, who would have opposed it, were at lunch; see M. G. Rogers, "Briggs: Conservative Heretic," 150.

16. John J. McCook, ed., *The Appeal in the Briggs Heresy Case before the General Assembly of the Presbyterian Church in the United States of America* (New York: John C. Rankin, 1893), 21.

17. Jeschke, "Briggs Case," 328.

18. Presbyterian Church in the U.S.A., *Minutes of the General Assembly,* 1893, 95–150; Jeschke, "Briggs Case," 330ff.

19. PCUSA, *Minutes of the General Assembly,* 1891, 93–105; Loetscher, *Broadening Church,* 55; M. G. Rogers, "Briggs: Conservative Heretic," 387.

20. Jeschke, "Briggs Case," 255; M. G. Rogers, "Briggs: Conservative Heretic," 403–4,

416, 430, 442–43; Hutchison, *Modernist Impulse in American Protestantism,* 178; Massa, "Briggs and Historical Criticism," 164; Charles A. Briggs, "Memorial to Thomas Hastings" (April 1911; in Briggs Papers, Union Theological Seminary, Box 22, Folder 15), 6–7.

21. *Minutes of the Synod of New York and Philadelphia*, 1758, 286.

22. Loetscher, *Broadening Church*, 63–68.

23. George L. Prentiss, *The Union Theological Seminary in the City of New York: Its Design and Another Decade of Its History* (Asbury Park, N.J.: Pennypacker, 1899), 339; Loetscher, *Broadening Church,* 71–74; M. G. Rogers, "Briggs: Conservative Heretic," 41; Henry Sloane Coffin, *A Half Century of Union Theological Seminary, 1896–1945: An Informal History* (New York: Charles Scribner's Sons, 1954), 103.

CHAPTER 2. TOO SMALL: THE PURE CONSERVATIVE CHURCH OF J. GRESHAM MACHEN

1. For an excellent treatment of the figures in this period, though one that comes to different conclusions than mine, see Bradley Longfield, *The Presbyterian Controversy: Fundamentalists, Modernists, and Moderates* (New York: Oxford University Press, 1991). See also Charles Allyn Russell, *Voices of American Fundamentalism: Seven Biographical Studies* (Philadelphia: Westminster Press, 1976), 144–45; George Marsden, *Fundamentalism and American Culture: The Shaping of Twentieth Century Evangelicalism, 1840–1925* (Oxford: Oxford University Press, 1980), 174–75. For the fullest treatment of Machen see Darryl G. Hart, *J. Gresham Machen* (Baltimore: Johns Hopkins University Press, 1994).

2. See, for example, J. Gresham Machen, "The Attack upon Princeton Seminary: A Plea for Fair Play" (Pamphlet published by the author, December 1927), 5.

3. J. Gresham Machen, *Christianity and Liberalism* (1923; Grand Rapids: Wm. B. Eerdmans Publishing Co., (1946), 20.

4. "Statement" to the Thompson Committee, 1926, 13–14. This idea is repeated in Machen's writings many times.

5. J. Gresham Machen, "The Responsibility of the Church in Our New Age," 1932, in Ned Stonehouse, ed., *What Is Christianity?* (Grand Rapids: Wm. B. Eerdmans Publishing Co., 1951), 284.

6. Machen, *Christianity and Liberalism,* 1923, 167–69.

7. For example, see ibid., 34; "The Present Issue in the Church," 1923, n.p.; "Prophets True and False," 1926, in Joseph F. Newton, ed., *Best Sermons 1926* (New York: Harcourt Brace), 129.

8. Machen, *Christianity and Liberalism*, 1923, 2.

9. Ibid., 160.

10. J. Gresham Machen, Letter to Clarence Macartney, May 5, 1936, in Machen Papers, Montgomery Library, Westminster Theological Seminary.

11. See Machen's comments after the 1929 General Assembly, quoted above.

12. Machen, Letter to S. M. Robinson, September 1, 1933; quoted in Wayne Headman, "A Critical Evaluation of J. Gresham Machen" (M. Theol. thesis, Princeton Theological Seminary, 1974), 167.

13. Machen, Letter to C. L. Richards, April 11, 1934; quoted in Headman, "Critical Evaluation," 164.

14. Machen, Letter to Arthur Machen, December 12, 1934; quoted in Headman, "Critical Evaluation," 197.

15. Machen, Letter to Clarence Macartney, May 9, 1936, 2, in Machen Papers, Montgomery Library, Westminster Theological Seminary.

16. Kenneth Cauthen, *The Impact of American Religious Liberalism* (New York: Harper & Row, 1962), 61–62.

17. Edwin H. Rian, *The Presbyterian Conflict* (Grand Rapids: Wm. B. Eerdmans Publishing Co., 1940), 29ff.

18. Marsden, *Fundamentalism and American Culture,* 172–73.

19. "An Affirmation," reprinted in Maurice W. Armstrong, Lefferts A. Loetscher, and Charles A. Anderson, eds., *The Presbyterian Enterprise: Sources of American Presbyterian History* (Philadelphia: Westminster Press, 1956), 287–88.

20. Machen, *Christianity and Liberalism,* 1923, 27.

21. See J. N. D. Kelly, *Early Christian Doctrines* (New York: Harper & Row, 1978), 375ff.

22. "An Affirmation," in Armstrong, Loetscher, and Anderson, *Presbyterian Enterprise,* 287.

23. Charles Evans Quirk, "Auburn Affirmation: A Critical Narrative of the Document Designed to Safeguard the Unity and Liberty of the Presbyterian Church in the United States of America in 1924" (Ph.D. diss., School of Religion, University of Iowa, 1967), 58, 177, 199–200, 382–83, 508, and 513–15.

24. Marsden, *Fundamentalism and American Culture*, 181; Quirk, "Auburn Affirmation," 157–58.

25. Henry Sloane Coffin, a leading liberal, sought to publicly distance the liberals from Erdman, in order that Erdman not be "tainted" in the eyes of conservatives. Quirk, "Auburn Affirmation," 242.

26. PCUSA, *Minutes of the General Assembly,* 1924, 195–96.

27. Rian, *Presbyterian Conflict,* 38. Fosdick remained an esteemed member of the Union Seminary faculty for years thereafter, and went on to be the founding pastor of Riverside Church, across the street from Union. He was arguably the leading liberal preacher in America in the first half of this century; in the estimation of Henry Sloane Coffin, Fosdick was "the most eminent preacher of his time." See Coffin, *Half Century of Union Seminary,* 62.

28. PCUSA, *Minutes of the General Assembly,* 1924, 198; Loetscher, *Broadening Church,* 123; Quirk, "Auburn Affirmation," 250–51.

29. D. Clair Davis, "Evangelicals and the Presbyterian Tradition: An Alternative Perspective," *Westminster Theological Journal,* 42, no. 1 (Fall 1979): 155–56.

CHAPTER 3. JUST RIGHT: THE LOYALIST CONSTITUTIONAL CHURCH OF THE SPECIAL COMMISSION OF 1925

1. Loetscher, *Broadening Church,* 128.

2. John F. Piper Jr., *Robert E. Speer: Prophet of the American Church* (Louisville, Ky.: Geneva Press, 2000); John H. Mackay, "Robert Elliott Speer, A Man of Yesterday and Tomorrow" (Pamphlet prepared for the Speer centennial celebration at Princeton Theological Seminary, 1967; in Robert Speer folder, H5, Department of History, Presbyterian Church (U.S.A.), 8.

3. Dale Soden, *The Reverend Mark Matthews: An Activist in the Progressive Era* (Seattle: University of Washington Press, 2001); Dr. Ezra Giboney and Agnes M. Potter, *The Life of Mark A. Matthews, "Tall Pine of the Sierras"* (Grand Rapids: Wm. B. Eerdmans Publishing Co., 1943), 93.

4. "Minutes of the Special Commission," meeting of September 22 to 24, 1925, 1, 6.

5. This position was argued forcefully by Machen, especially in his 1923 book *Christianity and Liberalism.*

6. "Report of the Committee on Causes of Unrest and Possibilities of Relief" (Presby-

terian Church in the U.S.A., Special Commission of 1925; Box M13.5 P92, Department of History, Presbyterian Church (U.S.A.)), 9.

7. Ibid., 8.

8. Ibid., 5.

9. Ibid., 6–7.

10. Ibid., 6.

11. "Report of the Committee on Constitutional Procedure" (Presbyterian Church in the U.S.A., Special Commission of 1925; Box M13.5 P92, Department of History, Presbyterian Church (U.S.A.)), 22.

12. Ibid., 27–28.

13. Presbyterian Church U.S.A., "Report of the Special Commission of 1925," 19–20.

14. Quirk, "Auburn Affirmation," 297.

15. Norman Furniss, *Fundamentalist Controversy, 1918–1931* (New Haven: Yale University Press, 1964), 137–38.

16. Ibid., 134; PCUSA, *Minutes of the General Assembly,*1927, 61; Loetscher, *Broadening Church*, 134.

17. J. Ross Stevenson, "Address to 1926 General Assembly," Papers of J. Ross Stevenson, Speer Library, Princeton Theological Seminary.

18. Stevenson, quoted in Russell, *Voices of Fundamentalism*, 155. Furniss reports that Erdman tried to "prevent open debate on the nomination to save Machen from sharp criticism by the liberals"; see Furniss, *Fundamentalist Controversy,* 140.

19. This division paralleled the distinction in local Presbyterian congregations between the session and the trustees.

20. See, for example, Stevenson's claim to be a "fundamentalist" and a "conservative Presbyterian," and that all of Princeton Seminary was loyal to the standards of the church. "The Greetings of a Conservative Presbyterian to the Methodist League for Faith and Life," 1926, Formal Address #202, Papers of J. Ross Stevenson, Speer Library, Princeton Theological Seminary.

21. PCUSA, *Minutes of the General Assembly,* 1929, 87.

22. John Hart, "The Controversy within the Presbyterian Church U.S.A., in the 1920s with Special Emphasis on the Reorganization of Princeton Theological Seminary" (Senior Thesis, Princeton University, 1978), 84.

23. Ibid., 88.

24. Russell, *Voices of Fundamentalism*, 155.

25. J. Gresham Machen, "Christian Scholarship and Evangelism," 1932, in Stonehouse, *What Is Christianity?*, 130–31.

26. PCUSA, *Minutes of the General Assembly*, 1933, 28.

27. Two other overtures were sent that were critical of the Board of Foreign Missions as well as four overtures commending it. Ibid., 154.

28. PCUSA, *Minutes of the General Assembly,* 1934, 71.

29. Ibid., 72.

30. PCUSA, *Minutes of the General Assembly*, 1933, 159.

31. Ibid., 159–60.

32. Rian, *Presbyterian Conflict*, 96.

33. PCUSA, *Minutes of the General Assembly*, 1934, 72.

34. Headman, "Critical Evaluation," 158.

35. PCUSA, *Minutes of the General Assembly,* 1934, 112.

36. Ibid., 115–16.

37. Rian, *Presbyterian Conflict*, 173, 175, 178–82.

38. Ibid., 184.

39. Presbytery of New Brunswick, "Action of the Presbytery of New Brunswick, April, 1935" (Typescript; Record Group 7, Box 1, Folder 3, Department of History, Presbyterian Church (U.S.A.), 4–6. See also Rian, *Presbyterian Conflict,* 184.

40. Rian, *Presbyterian Conflict,* 173–84; PCUSA, *Minutes of the General Assembly*, 1936, 101.

41. Presbyterian Church in the U.S.A., Publicity Department, "Statement" (Record Group 20, Box 1, Folder 9, Department of History, Presbyterian Church (U.S.A.), n.d., n.p.; *Minutes of the General Assembly*, 1936, 99–100.

42. Rian, *Presbyterian Conflict,* 219.

43. Ibid., 229.

44. Ibid., 260–65.

45. Dallas Roark, "J. Gresham Machen and His Desire to Maintain a Doctrinally True Presbyterian Church" (Ph.D. diss., State University of Iowa, 1963), 138.

46. Rian, *Presbyterian Conflict*, 103, 242.

CHAPTER 4. THE HALF-FINISHED STORY OF THE FIDELITY AND CHASTITY COMPETITION

1. United Presbyterian Church in the U.S.A. (UPCUSA), *Minutes of the General Assembly* (New York: Published by the Office of the General Assembly, 1970), 469.

2. UPCUSA, *Minutes of the General Assembly*, 1978, 265–66.

3. Ibid., 261.

4. Ibid., 263–64, 268.

5. UPCUSA *Minutes of the General Assembly*, 1982, 111.

6. Presbyterian Church in the U.S. (PCUS), *Minutes of the General Assembly* (Atlanta: Published by the Office of the General Assembly, 1977), 174.

7. PCUS, *Minutes of the General Assembly*, 1978, 190.

8. PCUS, *Minutes of the General Assembly*, 1979, 208.

9. PCUS, *Minutes of the General Assembly*, 1980, 213.

10. Presbyterian Church (U.S.A.) (PC(USA)), *Minutes of the General Assembly,* (Louisville, Ky.: Published by the Office of the General Assembly, 1987), 776.

11. PC(USA), *Minutes of the General Assembly*, 1991, 207.

12. Jerry Van Marter, "Panelists Say Homosexual Sex Wrong," Presbyterian News Service *General Assembly News* release, Jan. 2, 1990.

13. PC(USA), *Minutes of the General Assembly*, 1991, 263–350.

14. Ibid., 351–77.

15. Ibid., 958–91.

16. Ibid., 1019–20.

17. "The 203rd General Assembly of the Presbyterian Church (U.S.A.)," *Presbyterian Outlook*, June 24, 1991, 1–2.

18. PC(USA), *Minutes of the General Assembly,* 1991, 56.

19. Ibid., 61.

20. *Minutes of the General Assembly,* 1993, 166–70.

21. Ibid., 902–20, 926.

22. Ibid., 321.

23. Pamela Crouch, Presbyterian News Service *PC(USA) News* release, June 9, 1993.

24. PC(USA), *Minutes of the General Assembly,* 1993, 946.

25. Ibid., 77.

26. PC(USA), *Minutes of the General Assembly*, 1996, 175.

27. Ibid., 25.

28. Bill Lancaster, "Committee Sending 'Fidelity, Chastity' Amendment to GA," Presbyterian News Service *PC(USA) News* release, July 3, 1996.

29. See Gary Comstock, *Unrepentant, Self-Affirming, Practicing: Lesbian/Bisexual/Gay People within Organized Religion* (New York: Continuum, 1996), 54, 69.

30. PC(USA), *Minutes of the General Assembly*, 1996, 77–78.

31. Lancaster, *PC(USA) News* releases, July 6, 1996.

32. PC(USA), *Minutes of the General Assembly*, 1996, 79.

33. Ibid., 79.

34. Ibid., 98.

35. Fred Beuttler, "Repentance: The Intent of the Fidelity Amendment" (Typescript of a speech before Chicago Presbytery, January 14, 1997).

36. Eugene March, "The Whole Bible for the Whole Human Family: Members of the Biblical Faculty of the Presbyterian Seminaries Speak to the Issue of Ordination" (Photocopy, May 23, 1996).

37. Elizabeth Achtemeier and twenty-nine others, "Responsible Love: A Response to 'The Whole Bible for the Whole Human Family.' A Statement to the Commissioners to the 208th General Assembly, 1996." "Signed by Faculty Members of the Presbyterian Church (U.S.A.)" (Photocopy, 1996).

38. Presbyterian News Service, and Office of the General Assembly, PC(USA), *1997 Assembly in Brief,* Louisville, Ky., n.d. [July 1997].

39. Alexa Smith, "More Light Churches Network Supports Local Dissent Instead of a National Strategy on Gay and Lesbian Ordination," Presbyterian News Service 97239, June 4, 1997.

40. Jerry Van Marter, "Stated Clerk Says Covenants of Dissent, Withholding of Funds Are Irresponsible Tactics," Presbyterian News Service 97283, July 22, 1997.

41. Jerry Van Marter, " Covenant Network of Presbyterians Vows to Carry On," Presbyterian News Service 98380, Nov. 17, 1998.

42. Alexa Smith, "Results Not Official Yet, But Supporters and Opponents Agree Amendment A Is Lost," Presbyterian News Service 98095, March 18, 1998.

43. Jerry Van Marter, "Coalition, Covenant Network Leaders Call for 'Sabbatical' on Ordination Standards," Presbyterian News Service 98189, May 20, 1998.

44. Leslie Scanlon, "Churches Struggle in Pitching Big Tent," Presbyterian News Service 98229, July 27, 1998; reprinted with permission from *The* (Louisville, Ky.) *Courier-Journal.*

45. Alexa Smith, "Council Divided Against Itself Lets Stand an Award to a Lesbian Activist," Presbyterian News Service GA99003, June 18, 1999.

46. Bill Lancaster, "Assembly Opts for Unity/Diversity Dialogue, Not Another Amendment on Homosexual Issue," Presbyterian News Service GA99120, June 25, 1999.

47. Nancy Rodman, "Assembly Acts on Reparative Therapy, Other Issues," Presbyterian News Service GA99131, June 26, 1999.

48. Alexa Smith, "PJC Says Gay Man May Be Ordination Candidate, Ministers May Bless Same-Sex Unions: Panel delays decision whether Vermont church can defy ordination standards," Presbyterian News Service 00208, May 24, 2000.

49. Nancy D. Borst, "Assembly Concurs with Moratorium on Ordination and Sexuality: Committee gets overture to delay judicial actions," Presbyterian News Service GA00011, June 24, 2000.

50. Evan Silverstein and Jerry Van Marter, "81 Demonstrators Arrested during Soulforce Rally: General Assembly opening worship not disrupted," Presbyterian News Service GA00025, June 25, 2000.

51. Jerry Van Marter, "Assembly Sends Same Sex Union Ban Amendment to Presbyteries: Measure passes by 268–251 vote," Presbyterian News Service GA00150, June 30, 2000.

52. Jerry Van Marter, "Presbyterian Panel Survey: Most Presbyterians oppose same-sex unions: Meanwhile, with 73 percent of vote in, Amendment O trails, 53–74," Presbyterian News Service 01085, March 2, 2001.

53. Jerry Van Marter, "Vote on Same-Sex Union Amendment Will Be Close, Early Returns Indicate: Presbytery executives' 'third way' proposal gets mixed reaction," Presbyterian News Service 01024, Jan. 23, 2001.

54. Alexa Smith, "O-no Outcome Was an Accretion of Narrow Losses: In presbyteries, votes on sex issues are usually 50–50 (more or less)," Presbyterian News Service 01102, March 23, 2001.

55. Jerry Van Marter, "Stated Clerk Clarifies Status of Same-Sex Unions after Defeat of Amendment O: Same-sex union ceremonies must be distinct from marriage, Kirkpatrick says," Presbyterian News Service 01108, March 28, 2001.

56. Alexa Smith, "3 Conservative Credos Fuel Confessing 'Movement': Lay Committee version urges loyalty oath for church employees," Presbyterian News Service 01128, April 11, 2001.

57. Jerry Van Marter, "Assembly Sends Out an Amendment to Delete G-6.0106b: Proposal to open the way for gay ordination passes with 60% approval," Presbyterian News Service GA01151, June 15, 2001.

58. Jerry Van Marter, "PJC Rules Case of Gay Elder in Connecticut Is Moot: Osborne's 'seat on session has been filled,' so case is 'no longer relevant.'" Presbyterian News Service 01446, Dec. 4, 2001.

59. Jerry Van Marter, "Elders Support Rejection, Ministers Split on Amendment 01–A: Presbyterian Panel results suggest laity hold the balance of power in presbytery voting," Presbyterian News Service 01464, Dec. 18, 2001.

60. Jerry Van Marter, "Amendment A Is Defeated: Presbytery of South Louisiana casts 87th and deciding 'no' vote," Presbyterian News Service 02069, Feb. 19, 2002.

61. Jerry Van Marter, "Church Leaders Call for Reconciliation in Wake of Amendment 01–A's Defeat," Presbyterian News Service 02086, March 4, 2002.

62. John. A. Bolt and Leslie Scanlon, "The 70–30 Assembly: an analysis," *Presbyterian Outlook* Analysis, July 22–29, 2002.

CHAPTER 5. WHAT IS NORMAL IN THE PRESBYTERIAN CHURCH TODAY?

1. Data on Presbyterian seminarians and seminary graduates from Survey of Presbyterian Theological Institutions 1990, and Survey of Presbyterians at Non-Presbyterian Theological Seminaries 1990. Both are available through the American Religion Data Archive, www.thearda.com.

2. This table based on Presbyterian Panel data, 1994–96; other seminaries, producing small numbers of Presbyterian ministers, are omitted.

3. This last figure comes from the Presbyterian Panel, 1994–96.

4. This section is based on Presbyterian Panel 1994–96 data.

5. Alexa Smith, "Kirkpatrick Responds to Questions about Re-election Bid; Stated Clerk hopes greater unity will be his legacy," Presbyterian News Service 00235, June 15, 2000.

6. "Lay leaders" were defined by adding up an index that gave one point for each of the following: being an elder; serving on the session; serving on a congregational committee; chairing a congregational committee; being a trustee; being an officer of a congregational organization; being a church school teacher; being a church organist; serving on a presbytery, synod, or General Assembly committee; or having other leadership responsibilities in the church. Those with a score of five or higher, some 290 people altogether, are the "lay leaders" in this analysis.

7. The Panel does not ask the same kinds of involvement questions of the clergy, but a plausible approximation can be made by adding up their income, the size of the congregation they serve, whether they have an advanced theological degree, and what kind of job they have, ranging from senior pastor down to various part-time jobs. The highest-scoring group, 245 individuals, are here analyzed as "clergy leaders."

CHAPTER 6. PRACTICAL PRINCIPLES FOR A COMPETITIVE CHURCH

1. Trinterud, *Forming an American Tradition,* 49.
2. *Historical Sections of the Digest of the United Presbyterian Church of North America and Presbyterian Church in the United States of America to May 27, 1958* (Published for the Office of the General Assembly by the Board of Christian Education of the United Presbyterian Church in the U.S.A., Philadelphia), 1287–88.
3. Ibid., 1288. The one minister who was not ready to subscribe that day did so the next year.
4. Charles Hodge, *The Constitutional History of the Presbyterian Church in the United States of America: Part I, 1705 to 1741* (Philadelphia: William S. Martien, 1839), 150.
5. Briggs, *American Presbyterianism,* 121.
6. *Historical Sections of the Digest,* 1289.
7. Briggs, *American Presbyterianism,* 318.
8. Charles Hodge, *The Constitutional History of the Presbyterian Church in the United States of America: Part II, 1741 to 1788* (Philadelphia: William S. Martien, 1840), 377.
9. *Historical Sections of the Digest,* 1310; see also *The Constitution of the Presbyterian Church (U.S.A.),* Part II, *Book of Order 2001–2002* (Louisville, Ky.: Published by the Office of the General Assembly), G-6.0108b, n. 1.
10. Briggs, *American Presbyterianism,* 370–71.
11. Loetscher, *Brief History,* 69–70, 80, and 92–104; Trinterud, *Forming an American Tradition,* 95ff.
12. "[I]n the South the debates were short-lived, because dissent was simply not tolerated." Marsden, *Fundamentalism and American Culture,* 103.
13. George Marsden, *The Evangelical Mind and the New School Presbyterian Experience: A Case Study of Thought and Theology in Nineteenth Century America* (New Haven: Yale University Press, 1970), 228.
14. For examples of this misunderstanding, see my "The Presbyterian Controversy: Triumph of the Loyalist Center," in Douglas Jacobsen and William Vance Trollinger Jr., eds., *Re-Forming the Center: American Protestantism, 1900 to the Present* (Grand Rapids: Wm. B. Eerdmans Publishing Co., 1998), 122 n. 28.
15. Presbyterian Church U.S.A., "Report of the Special Commission of 1925," 19–20.
16. "Studies in the Constitution of the Presbyterian Church in the U.S.A.," *Minutes of the General Assembly,* 1934, 73–74.
17. Ibid., 76–77.
18. Alexa Smith, "'Take a Hike' Overtures Draw Battle Lines Between Liberals, Conservatives—and Conservatives," Presbyterian News Service 00028, Jan. 21, 2000.

19. "113 Presbytery Executives Call for a Way out of Sexuality Debates That Is Not Legislative or Judicial," Presbyterian News Service 00464, Dec. 21, 2000.

20. John Filiatreau, "Peacemakers Explore Non-Christian Faith Traditions: 600 Presbyterians Share 'Holy Ghost Good Time' in Sunny California." Presbyterian News Service 00274, Aug. 2, 2000.

21. Alexa Smith, "GAC Executive Admits Initial Response to Ficca Controversy Was 'Inadequate': Detterick says GAC will review policies for choosing conference speakers." Presbyterian News Service 00391, Nov. 2, 2000.

22. www.confessingchurch.homestead.com.

23. Bill Lancaster, "Assembly Rejects Declaration of Irreconcilable Impasse, New Abortion Study," Presbyterian News Service GA00128, June 29, 2000.

24. Bill Lancaster, "Moderator Says His Greatest Task Is to Pursue Reconciliation," Presbyterian News Service GA00022, June 24, 2000.

25. "GA Moderator Calls for a 'Commission' to Seek Reconciliation, Unity: Rhee endorses proposal to pursue 'a more excellent way.'" Presbyterian News Service 01170, May 14, 2001.

26. Bill Lancaster, "Rhee, Detterick, Kirkpatrick Support Formation of Commission: Leaders advance idea of writing a new confession," Presbyterian News Service GA01034, June 11, 2001.

27. Bill Lancaster, "Assembly Approves Task Force to Seek Peace, Unity and Purity of the Church," Presbyterian News Service GA01116, June 13, 2001.

28. Jerry Van Marter, "Three Moderators Announce 21-Member Theological Task Force: Gary Demarest, Jenny Stoner to serve as co-moderators," Presbyterian News Service 01366, Oct. 4, 2001.

29. This section is based on the press release announcing the task force, supplemented by my conversations with task force members at their third meeting in Lisle, Illinois, in August 2002.

30. Jerry Van Marter, "Peace, Unity and Purity Task Force Gets Under Way; Group forges covenant for its work, opts for consensus decision-making style," Presbyterian News Service 01455, Dec. 10, 2001.

31. I am grateful to Janice Catron for that formulation.

32. I am grateful to Barbara Wheeler and Jack Haberer for this characterization.

33. "General Assembly Focus Discussion Groups," 8; emphasis in original.

CHAPTER 7. A MODEST PROPOSAL: PRESBYTERS RULE!

1. *Book of Order* G-2.0100.

2. James Moorhead, "Redefining Confessionalism: American Presbyterians in the Twentieth Century," in Milton J. Coalter, John M. Mulder, and Louis B. Weeks, eds., *The Confessional Mosaic: Presbyterians and Twentieth-Century Theology,* Presbyterian Presence (Louisville, Ky.: Westminster/John Knox Press, 1990).

3. "The Confession of 1967 and the Book of Confessions." *Network News*, 22, no. 2 (spring 2002).

4. *Historical Sections of the Digest,* 1287–88.

5. *Book of Order* G-14.0207.

6. I am grateful to Fred Beuttler for this point.

7. Kirkpatrick and Hopper, *What Unites Presbyterians*, 80.

8. *Book of Order* G-2.0200.

9. I am grateful to Rodney Hunter for pushing this point, and only wish I had a more satisfactory answer.

10. Clifton Kirkpatrick, "The Role of the *Constitution* in the Life of the Church," An Address at Columbia Theological Seminary, April 26, 2002.

11. *Book of Order* G-9.0103.

12. Kirkpatrick and Hopper, *What Unites Presbyterians*, 114.

13. William Chapman, *History and Theology in the Book of Order: Blood on Every Page* (Louisville, Ky.: Witherspoon Press, 1999), 77.

14. Frank Buhrman, "Presbyterian? You Could Be a Redneck–and That's Good, Coalition Speaker Says," Presbyterian News Service GA02051, June 18, 2002.

15. Jack Rogers, *Reading the Bible and the Confessions: The Presbyterian Way* (Louisville, Ky.: Geneva Press, 1999), 104–5.

16. Lois Boyd and R. Douglas Brackenridge, *Presbyterian Women in America: Two Centuries of a Quest for Status,* Presbyterian Historical Society Contributions to the Study of Religion No. 9 (Westport, Conn.: Greenwood Press, 1983), 235.

17. Personal communication from a denominational official, 2002.

18. *Book of Order*, G-14.0208b.

19. Rodney Stark and Roger Finke, *The Churching of America, 1776–1990* (New Brunswick, N.J.: Rutgers University Press, 1992), 86.

20. "It is the duty both of private Christians and societies to exercise mutual forbearance toward each other." *Book of Order* G-1.0305.

21. J. Rogers, *Claiming the Center,* 7.

22. Ibid., 63–64.

23. Haberer, *GodViews,* 29.

APPENDIX

1. Liberals are almost twice as likely to get A's as conservatives are.

2. Austin, Columbia, Louisville, Presbyterian School of Christian Education, Johnson C. Smith, Union in Virginia.

3. A member of the northern Presbyterian Church, prior to the 1983 reunion.

4. On a five-point scale, from 1 = "the Bible is inerrant in all details" to 5 = "the Bible should be read in historical context," those answering 5.

5. On a five-point scale, from 1 = "God is transcendent" to 5 = "God is immanent," those answering 2, 3, or 4.

6. On a five-point scale, from 1 = "Not strongly committed to the denominational system" to 5 = "Strongly committed to the denominational system," those answering 5.

7. On a seven-point theological spectrum, those answering 3, 4, or 5.

8. Staff have no conservatives.

9. Includes "neo-orthodox."

10. Includes "neo-orthodox."

11. On a five-point scale, from 1 = "the Bible is inerrant in all details" to 5 = "the Bible should be read in historical context," only those answering 5.

12. On a five-point scale, from 1 = "God is transcendent" to 5 = "God is immanent," those answering 2, 3, 4.

13. Includes "neo-orthodox."

14. Includes "neo-orthodox."

15. Want to be a governing body executive in ten years = 15%.

16. 70% at non-Presbyterian seminaries wish to have a doctorate in ten years.

17. A member of the northern Presbyterian Church, prior to the 1983 reunion.

18. Austin, Columbia, Louisville, Presbyterian School of Christian Education, Johnson C. Smith, Union in Virginia.

19. On a five-point scale, from 1 = "Not strongly committed to the denominational system" to 5 = "Strongly committed to the denominational system," those answering 5.

20. On a seven-point theological spectrum, those answering 3, 4, or 5.

21. Includes 48% at non-Presbyterian seminaries who call themselves "evangelical."

22. Described their theological position as "very conservative."

23. Described their theological position as "very liberal."

24. Clergy on presbytery, synod, or national church staffs.

25. Nearly all Presbyterian clergy are college graduates. This number represents those with advanced theological degrees (D.Min., S.T.D., Th.D., Ph.D.). This compares to a normal rate for all Presbyterian clergy of 25 percent.

26. See note 25.

27. This question was only asked of members and elders.

28. No staff members describe their political orientation as conservative or very conservative.

29. Lay leaders' second choice was that the congregation was spiritually alive.

30. Far rights' top two reasons for joining their congregation: meaningful sermons and it was the closest Presbyterian church.

31. Far rights' second choice was that they enjoyed the worship; "prefer the Presbyterian Church" was their eighth choice.

32. Far lefts' second choice was "God is at work here"; "prefer the Presbyterian Church" was their fifth choice.

33. This question was not asked of clergy. This number refers to a comparable question, asking if clergy spent at least three hours per month reaching out to the unchurched. The norm for all Presbyterian clergy is 48 percent.

34. See note 33.

35. Clergy leaders' second most important faith claim was the importance of religion in their life; Christ as their savior was a close third.

36. Far lefts' second most important belief was in helping others; that Christ is their savior was their eighth choice.

37. Clergy staffs' second most important faith claim was the importance of religion in their life; Christ as their savior was sixth choice.

38. Clergy leaders' second favorite use for churchwide offerings is new church development.

39. Clergy leaders' second least favorite use for churchwide offerings is spiritual growth.

40. Far lefts' second least favorite use for churchwide offerings is to promote church unity.

41. Clergy staffs' second least favorite use for churchwide offerings is spiritual growth.

Index